BARRIERS OF IBS IN

MALAYSIA

Saeed Kamankesh

Title: BARRIERS OF IBS IN MALAYSIA
Author: Saeed Kamankesh
ISBN: 9781939123022
Library Congress Control Number (LCCN): 2014922128
Publisher: Supreme Century, Los Angeles, CA, USA
Prepare for Publishing: Asan Nashr

ACKNOWLEDGMENT

First of all I am grateful to God who gives me sound mine & sound health to accomplish my project. I would like to express my deepest gratitude to my research Supervisor Mr.Kumarason Rasiah for his support and guidance throughout the research as well as our deputy dean Mdm.Hemawathi who gave me the golden opportunity to do this wonderful project on the topic of Barriers of IBS in Malaysia which also helped me in doing a lot of research and I came to know about so many new things I am really thankful to them.

Secondly I would also like to thanks my parents who supported me a lot to finishing this project within the limited time. Actually it was not possible for me to complete a server task without such help. I am making this project not only for marks but to also increase my knowledge.

Thanks again to all who helped me.

ABSTRACT

Industrialized Building System (IBS) were introduced to Malaysia to solve issues associated with dependencies of foreign workers, raising demand of affordable accommodations and improving image, quality and productivity of construction industry. This research is to highlights the current development of IBS in Malaysian construction industry and potential challenges related to the implementation of IBS. The objectives of the research are to identify the readiness of adapting IBS; determine the barriers in the implementation of IBS; and identify ways to enhance it. Questionnaires survey was conducted in order to achieve the objectives. The respondents consisted of architects, contractors, developers, consultants and quantity surveyors. The data were tabulated using Microsoft Excel and then analyzed using average index. In conclusion, the barriers of IBS in Malaysia has been identified and discussed. According to this research, technical limitation, lack of standardization and price of IBS are the main barriers in IBS implementation in Malaysia.

Table of Contents

List of Figures

List of Tables

List of Chart

List of Bar Chart

INTRODUCTION

1.1 Introduction

Malaysia is recognized for its future policies and strategies in an effort to global participation in all aspects of the industry. Being a worldwide player in field of construction needs significant hard work in adopt technologies with high quality and new systems with both developed and developing countries. The achievement of these hard work will allow us to break through the worldwide market and export our construction expertise and qualified at the same time increase our own domestic management and development.

To accelerate national economic activities and increase growth, the construction industry plays a vital role in the Government's attempts. It is consequently essential for the sector to constantly embark on measures to improve effectiveness, productivity and quality. In the direction of this end, the use of IBS or known as Industrialized Building Systems is the correct movement in realizing this purpose.

Industrialized Building Systems promises prominent levels of expertise right through the industry, from planners, installers, manufacturers, designers, engineers, and developers. The reimbursement of Industrialized Building Systems is various and far off reaching. Reduced the wastage with better site of management and trim down construction time is a few of these reimbursement, that will eventually produce the surpass products for the inhabitants. Without a doubt with better quality, productivity and safety, IBS or Industrialized Building Systems will play a part towards a change for the better construction industry, in addition to enhance the worldwide competitiveness of Malaysian builders.

1.2 Background

The construction industry represents a vital component of Malaysian economy. Even though it report for no more than 2.8 percent of the GDP or Gross Domestic Product in 2008 fourth quarter, the industry is vital to countrywide growth as it has the straight effects to the

1

financial system of the country. The construction industry as well endows with employment chance for roughly 800,000 people, based from CIMP 2006-2015. In 1987, concur to Wang the construction industry is able to serve up as a gauge in indicating the Countrywide's economic circumstances.

Vigorous construction activities normally show that the Countrywide's economy is thriving and progressing well, and while lethargic construction activities explain that the Countrywide's economy situation is beneath depression.

According the report from CIDB years 2003, it also highlight the assistance from the construction sector are over simply economic, superior building and infrastructure construction in which the products are made directly or indirectly has contributed extensively to the wealth creation and quality of life of residents. Balanced economic activity in Malaysia will be automatically created as a result of construction activities which in turn will create more industrial productivity

Construction industry principally consists of a range of processes; occupy many parties and diverse stages of work. This is occupying the participation of different parties from different sectors in demand to make sure the effectiveness of the construction work implementation. The effectiveness and achievement of construction improvement and activities depends a great deal on the excellence of organizational and managerial presentation plus the effectual organization via good cooperation from the various parties. It is consequently noticeable that the improvements of the construction industry know how to merely be achieved if each team members take part in effectual roles within their work.

Nevertheless, plan the future development of the construction industry of Malaysia is not in accordance with the conditions of the existing local industry, this is due to the difference in work efficiency, work quality and productivity challenges that occur areas. Currently, the construction industry still uses the services of intensive and low technology as a method of construction. The use of intensive labour of foreign workers who do not have the expertise and low-tech equipment as well as construction methods that are outdated, will ultimately lead to low productivity and work efficiency on the construction site. As a result, this will lead to practices that are not productive and will contribute to the delivery of the work.

According to Ismail, in 2001, there were 800,000 housing units planned and in addition to these figures there are as many as 585,000 units or 73.1 percent planned to house a low price and the middle class in the 7th Malaysia Plan. Disappointing fact is that only 20 percent can be achieved from the overall total target when lots of incentives and promotions are being made to encourage developers venturing into the housing.

It is eagerly awaited by the citizens of Malaysia, especially for those who are lower-middle income residents brought by Walled et al. in 2003, which has given the announcement of the 8th Malaysia Plan with planning a cheap house lower to the middle as much as 600,000 to 800,000 in the whole of Malaysia. This is a difficult task to achieve these targets given the conventional systems currently being practiced extensively in the Malaysian construction industry.

Consequently, the confront the IBS or Industrialized Building System is to create an environment that promises to lower the construction costs, increase productivity and meet the level of demand for housing at an affordable price. In principle, the current trend awareness, innovation and the latest construction technologies is very important in order to survive in a highly competitive market

1.3 Problem Statement

Malaysia is a country of destination countries to work by many foreigners, so do not be surprised if we see a lot of foreign citizens who depend on this neighboring country. Low wages are given to these foreign workers, and it is this which is widely used by many of the construction industry in Malaysia. The construction industry in Malaysia almost entirely dominated by foreign workers who obviously do not have specific skills in the field of construction industry. This situation is very worrying for the future period. This has been alluded to in the IBS Roadmap 2003-2010, the main problems existing in the construction industry in Malaysia is the dependence on foreign labor.

Foreign workers are unskilled has given a lot of serious problems such as low quality of work, delays, social issues, waste, disease, and others. This makes the local workforce cannot compete with foreign workers because their wages are very low. The low awareness of safety and health at work in the construction industry has managed to create a 3D image that is difficult, dangerous and dirty. However, it is not without a solution. Use of Industrialized building systems proved to be very effective in the construction industry, because it can increase productivity, minimize waste, better quality, faster turnaround and use less labor. In addition, safe and clean, because the components of prefabricated offsite mechanically installed using a crane on site using only a minimal amount of workers, which is will leave the construction site with more neat and clean.

Although all of the support and the benefits provided by the government, but an attempt at using IBS in the construction industry in Malaysia still very low compared to conventional systems. Indifference is done almost all by the industry stakeholders have made it difficult to develop the system even though the development of ideas is open widely. This could be because the resistance will change and the information is not sufficient to support the feasibility of the change. Fees for foreign workers who have made the relatively low local contractors are reluctant to switch to using IBS. IBS Adoption in Malaysia is now more in the direction of client-driven rather than consumer driven measure up to developed countries.

1.4   Aim and Objectives of the Study

The purpose of this study was to investigate and determine the presence of obstacles in the implementation of the system of industrial development in the construction industry in Malaysia. In order to achieve the desired result of this research, this study has the following specific objectives:

1. To determine the readiness of contractors and designers to adapt Industrialized Building Systems that will apply to their construction projects.
2. To determine the presence of obstacles in the application of Industrialized Building Systems in the construction industry in Malaysia.
3. as a measure to improve the implementation of Industrialized Building Systems in the construction industry.

1.5   Scope of the Study and Limitations

In order to achieve the objectives of this study, the scope of the study will only focus on the development of the construction industry that took place in Malaysia. Focus on the construction industry in Malaysia will provide a clearer view of the ongoing overall development that exists in the local industry. The study will be limited to development projects that have used the Industrialized Building Systems since so far only Industrialized Building Systems is occupied in structural steel and precast elements.

Some barriers are highlighted and input has been obtained from the questionnaire study is based on a review of previous studies that focus on the same area. The respondents of the questionnaire are mainly composed of developers, contractors, developers, quantity surveyors, architects and consultants in Malaysia. This survey aims to determine the readiness of the construction industry players to work together with the Industrialized Building System and find bottlenecks in the application of advanced Industrialized Building Systems in the construction industry in Malaysia.

The results of the analysis are not representative of the entire construction industry in Malaysia because it is based on the respondents of the questionnaire data alone. After all, the discussions are based on a comparison of data analysed and the information from the literature. The resulting conclusion is based on the research objectives.

1.6   Significance of the study

At present the major challenges in Malaysia's about construction industry is require of innovation and enthusiasm as the workforce is aging and dwindling as gradually less young come into the industry. If the facts were already evident is allowed to continue, the construction industry will fall into a very worrying situation, especially with the condition of dependence on foreign labour, no modernization in industrial engineering as well as the lack of adequate technology. Hence the evolution of industrial technology and industrialization methods of building construction is needed.

The ability to determine the barriers that hinder the development of IBS in Malaysian construction industry is the first stage in the implementation of IBS in a row. It is very important to know because if there obstacles in the implementation of IBS then it would make it easier to figure out solutions and ways of solving the problem.

1.6   Research Questions

In order to keep on focus the area of research and the presentation of the report, it is very important to develop the questions for research. Here are a few research questions that arise when doing research:

- ☐   What are the challenges and problems in construction industry?
- ☐   What is the concern in present improvement of IBS in Malaysian construction industry?
- ☐   What are the obstacles that arise in the implementation of IBS in the construction industry in Malaysia?
- ☐   What kind of information to be composed?
- ☐   How to bring out the survey?
- ☐   Who were the respondents?
- ☐   How to use data that has been collected?

1.7   Research Methodology

To meet the requirements of the purpose of this study, the method of investigation has been carried out which includes data collection methods such as case studies, the study documents, data collection and preparation of the questionnaire. The procedure for the study research as shown in Figure 1.1.

1.8   Structure of Report

The report on the study consists of five chapters in which the content of each chapter is as follows:

Chapter 1 is the introduction to the report. This section serves to provide a full overview of the entire report. Chapter 1 consists of the introduction and followed by a statement of the problem, the objective, and continued to the scope of the study, then the significance of the research, research questions, as well as research methodology and report structure.

Chapter 2 is part of the literature review is based on findings from a variety of different sources such as books, research papers, journals, technical papers, etc.. Chapter 2 contains definitions, categorization of building system and Industrialized Building System, important characteristic of Industrialized Building System, advantages and shortcomings of Industrialized Building System, knowledge's and accomplishment of Industrialized Building System in other countries, Industrialized Building System in Malaysia, Industrialized Building System Roadmap, obstacle of Industrialized Building System in Malaysia and CIMP or Construction Industry Master Plan 2006-2015.

Chapter 3 describes in detail about the research methodology includes questionnaires, questionnaire preparation and review of the literature along with methods of analysis.

Chapter 4 analyses the data using frequency analysis and average index to conduct a questionnaire survey. Chapter 4 also discusses in detail about the data are analysed and the findings are discussed.

Chapter 5 to evaluate whether the research objectives have been achieved or not, highlights the findings and provide overall study conclusions on the subject.

Figure 1. 1 Research flow chart

Recommendations for further study included in this chapter.

LITERATURE REVIEW

2.1 Definitions

Awaiting the current time there has been no solitary normally accepted description of Industrialized Building System. Industrialized Building System can be numerous things to various industry players. Nevertheless, there are numerous descriptions from further researchers that expose the concept of Industrialized Building System which extensively acknowledged by the construction industry.

In an early literature, Dietz in 1971 has defined Industrialized Building System as "It is a combination of all components and subsystems in the overall process that fully utilize the production process, transport and assembly of industrial engineering called the total integration".

In the meantime Junid in 1986 described Industrialized Building System as "development by which elements of building are visualized, planned and formulated, conveyed and stiffed at site. The system contains steadiness mixture among software and hardware part. The software aspect consist of system design, which is multifaceted procedure of studying the necessity of the end user, market investigation and the expansion of standardize element".

Parid in 1997 defines Industrialized Building System as "systems which utilize the techniques of industrial production in both the production and assembly of components of the building, or it could be both".

An Interpretation of Esa et al in 1998 explains that Industrialized Building System is a "continuum begins with utilizing craftsmen for every aspect of the construction so that the system can take advantage of manufacturing production to minimize any waste of resources and to increase the value of the end user".

Meanwhile, Warszawski in 1999 describes Industrialized Building System as "a set of

8

elements that are related to each other and act together in carrying out the designated performance of buildings". In the same year, Trikha add definitions of Industrialized Building System which is a system in which the components are prefabricated concrete in a property or an assembly plant that forms a structure with a minimum construction.

Lessing et al in 2005 defines Industrialized Building System as developed that has been incorporated as well as from end to end the construction progression next to the association that has been arrangement for more well-organized management enhancement, systematize and manage the assets used, evaluate the activities and outcomes are sustained by the utilize of diverse component progress.

Rahman et al in 2006 have defined Industrialized Building System as a construction system that is built using pre-fabricated components. In this case the components of the manufacturing process will be carried out systematically by using machine, formworks and other shapes in the form of mechanical equipment. The components are manufactured offsite once completed will be sent to the construction site to be continued into the assembly process.

Almost all explanation of Industrialized Building System mention the word prefabricated, off-site production and mass production of building components intended as a primary characteristic of Industrialized Building System. The scope of Industrialized Building System itself focuses on the construction of the building rather than civil or structural engineering projects. As a conclusion of these results, it is most appropriate if the Industrialized Building System is defined referring to CIDB Malaysia in 2001 is said to be a construction system in which the components are manufactured done at the factory, either offsite or onsite, positioned and assembled into the structure in place to minimize the additional activities.

2.2   Classification of Building System

In 1977, Majzub propose a concept within the classification of a building system in which to construct a classification that consists of the skeletal system, the system panel and box systems as presented in Table 2.1. Should use the relative weights of the components that serve as the main basis. Factor weights have a significant impact on the transportation components and also affect the production method and the method of mounting components on site. This method has a major drawback which cannot be combined with other methods of building systems that are currently being developed in Malaysia, so it would be difficult if it is still the case in Malaysia.

Table 2. 1 Kinds of materials

No.	General System	System	Production Material
1	Frame system	Light weight frame	Wood, light gage metals
		Medium light weig frame	Metal, reinforced plastic laminated wood
		Heavy weight frame	Heavy steel, concrete
2	Panel system	Light and medium weight panel	Wood frame, metal frame ar composite material
		Heavy weight panel (factory produced)	Tangible
		Heavy weight panel (tilt up-produced on sit	Tangible
3	Box system (modules)	Medium weight box (mobile)	Wood frame, light gage met composite
		Medium weight box (sectional)	Wood frame, light gage met composite
		Heavy weight box (factory produced)	Tangible
		Heavy box (tunnel produced on site)	Tangible

A few years later, in 1998 Badir proposed type of existing building systems in Malaysia under the name Badir-Razali. Types of building systems are classified into four types, namely conventional systems, prefabricated systems, Cast-in Situ systems and composite building system shown in Figure 2.1. Each building system will be represented by their own construction methods are further marked with geometry, construction technology and functional configurations.

Figure 2. 1 Types of construction system according to Badir-Razali categorization in Malaysia (By Badir in 1998)

Depend on the meticulous attention of their customers and manufacturers. His categorization uses construction technology as a source for classifying different building systems. In this method four main factions can be eminent such as scheme using steel, cast in situ tangible, timber and precast material as their major structural as well as break enclosing materials. These structures can be advance classified according to geometrical patterns of their major framing mechanism that are the linear or outline (rays and columns) system, planar or pane system and three dimensional or package systems.

2.3   Classification of IBS

In Malaysia, in 2003 CIDB Industrialized Building System has made a classification into five categories, namely steel formwork system, precast concrete panels and framing system box, steel frame systems, system block work and timber frame systems. Industrialized Building System is a construction process that is carried out by making use of the products, techniques, components or building systems which involve prefabricated components and on-site installation. From the type of structural classification, there are five major groups in Industrialized Building System commonly used in Malaysia as shown in the following sub-sections, which are mainly based on the classification performed by the CIDB with a few modifications.

2.3.1 Precast Concrete Systems

Precast Concrete Systems here is definite as some precast mechanism that is used in construction industry. Precast Concrete Systems are incorporated all category of precast concrete systems as definite at earlier research, which exposed in Figure 2.2 to 2.4 integrated as tag along:

1. 1.　　　Precast concrete panel, framing and box systems

　　.　　　Precast concrete wall system

2. 3.　　　Construction with precast concrete slab

The precast concrete framed system as exposed in Figure 2.2 is one of the mainly accepted forms of IBS or industrialized building system. The precast concrete framed construction consists of block, ray and column element that are made-up or artificial offsite by machine with formwork. The benefit of the system is far above the ground level of suppleness in expression of larger obvious detachment between columns, as an effect longer width give superior open space and better self-determination of areas.

Figure 2. 2 Prefabricated framing, concrete box system and the panel. (NFPA 2004 images)

Precast concrete wall system that consists of a structural framework of the building is made of pre-cast slab with a load bearing wall. The load bearing walls and slabs through the production process off-site and transported to a place that will be built. These systems are more widely used because it is not complicated and quite simple with a lower degree of flexibility, while the elimination of load bearing walls are restricted for use. With detailed design and well established coordination between advertisers and designers, installation can be done very quickly with the number of wet trades location can be reduced to a minimum.

Figure 2. 3 Precast concrete wall system (NFPA pictures, 2004)

Due to integrate precast concrete frame system with precast concrete, the building is also referred to as a hybrid construction. Building construction consists of a combination hybrid frame with precast concrete core slab, also called precast hollow boards. It has become very popular among builders because the resulting benefits are speed and high quality of precast concrete are combined with flexibility, economic benefits, and also the stability properties of monolithic structural framing systems both with cast concrete and steel framing systems in situ, which in building will finally provide a highly practical and efficient.

Figure 2. 4 Building with precast concrete slab (Tekla pictures)

2.3.2 Steel Formwork System

The system is included in the category of IBS or Industrialized Building System because the construction process is done by using a systematic method and mechanics by using steel formwork panels can be reused. This system allows rapid placement of concrete cast in place situ to form slabs, columns, beams and walls. This system will be a better choice to make wall construction instead of columns and beams for numerous repetitive elements related wall on the building wall portal. Steel formworks elements are usually obtainable in typical panel dimensions and stiffened by built in stiffeners or fasten rods to refuse to accept lateral concrete heaviness through concreting. It recommends faster speed of installation, moderately lower cost and minimalism in equipment. It moreover offers good exactness and smooth inside finishing that get rid of require of plastering. Illustration of steel formwork system is as exposed in Figure 2.5.

Figure 2. 5 PERI TRIO Steel Formwork System (PERI Formwork System Inc.

2.3.3 Steel-framed building and Roof Trusses

In 2009, Sufian explained that steel is a material that is very rigid and strong matching when used in construction and as a reparative frame building with architectural details that have a very high flexibility in providing long coverage of structures. It is often used in the frame for building high-rise, poor construction and roof construction. The advantages of using a steel frame system as shown in Figure 2.6 is the speed of the larger building and construction of a much more minimalist and simple, and durable long enough so it is suitable if used in the construction of tall buildings. Lately steel roof truss is widely used in various types of housing for very competitive prices compared with a wooden roof truss. *Figure 2. 6 Typical project with steel framing system (By Sufian, 2009)*

2.3.4 Prefabricated Timber Framing System

In the early 1970s, single storey terrace houses at bargain prices mostly built using wood framing and plain boards placed on the three-meter wall plastered by taking advantage of a simple raft foundation for the structure of the resulting super light. Figure 2.7 shows the construction of housing at low prices developed in rural or remote town. Nowadays the type of this construction has been included in the classification as one of the Industrialized Building System.

Figure 2. 7 Characteristic project with timber forming system (By Sufian, 2009)

Prefabricated wood framing systems are generally used in the context of a conventional roof and a wooden frame. Wood is the way of combining them into prefabricated truss members by utilizing steel plate. Because wood is vulnerable to pests, it is important to provide a chemical disinfectant to all products made from wood. Then, the installation carried out at the site by bringing together the prefabricated roof truss so that the stronger the roof beams.

On the other hand the practices of timber for Industrialized Building System give the impression impractical in this period. In reality, the points of view towards such achievement grow to be not as good as when the cost of timber rose lately. The major cause for choosing timber is presently because of its litheness, conservative and economic motivations.

2.3.5 Block Work System

Referring to the statement Sufian in 2009, these systems depend on the dimensions of the existing modular in design stage, which is identical with the Lego blocks to a considerable scope. Moreover, it applies weight bearing walls (as exposed in Figure 2.8) as a result of incorporating the columns along with the beams as fundamental fraction of the walls in support of all house category. The components of block work system consist of intertwine concrete building material units along with lightweight concrete blocks. The components are fabricated plus cured in the industrial unit. The components are usually worn as bricks in constructions along with interlocking material block concrete. Depends on the plan, the total that can be saved on top of a wall can be very variety starting flanked by 10 percent up to 30 percent in the midst of financial compensation such as up to 30 percent reduction in wall construction, quicker in project achievement, no beam along with column, a lesser amount of foundation cost.

Figure 2. 8 Characteristic project using block work system (By Sufian, 2009)

2.4   Essential Characteristics of IBS

Thanoon et al in 2003 sharp out some of the crucial characteristics which reveal unbeaten implementations of industrialized building system are temporarily discussed as tag along:

2.4.1   Closed System

A closed system is classified into two categories, the first is production based on clients design and the second design is based on the pre-production of the caster. The first category is specifically designed to meet the spatial needs of clients which require different functions within the architectural design of the building and has a much more specific. Client needs is paramount in the design of temporary pre-caster has a tendency to produce a specific component for building.

Meanwhile, in 1999 Warszawski a statement that production using the base as pre design scope in designing, building or group of components to produce a uniform type of building that can later be manufactured using a variety of common components. However, setting the type of building can be economically justified if it has a condition like this.

a. a.   Project size large enough to distribute the design and production costs will be charged an additional fee per component for a particular design.

b. b.   The architectural design examines large repetitive component and consistency. In reverence to this, a new prefabrication system can triumph over the prerequisite of various standardized components by mechanize the design and manufacture process.

c. c.   There is a plenty order for a typical category of building such as school so that a bunch production can be acquired.

d. d.   There is a severe advertising strategy through pre-caster to make clear to the clients and designer the prospective advantage of the structure in term of economics along with noneconomic features.

2.4.2 Open Building System (OBS)

In observation of the boundaries inbuilt in the closed system, OBS or known as Open Building System consent to bigger litheness of design along with maximum synchronization flanked by the designer along with pre-caster has been propositioned. Thanoon *et al* in 2003 was said that Open Building System permits the pre-caster to create a limited number of components with a programmed variety of product plus at the same time keep up architectural aesthetic importance.

Open Building System facilitates openness in its organization supplier where all and sundry can propose to make lower price. In adding up, the pre-caster along with erectors will look in favor of collaboration models that will produce win-win circumstances for mutually parties. Thanoon *et al* in 2003 supplementary that Open Building System or OBS gives a high degree of design litheness, which necessary an utmost coordination flanked by the designer along with pre-caster.

In spite of countless benefits inbuilt in Open Building System, its acceptance occurrences are one of the main setbacks. For instance, combined and correlation problem take place when

16

two factors from dissimilar system are unchanging together. This is for the reason that similar correlation technology have to be observed in order to attain greater structural presentation. However, Open Building System in addition lets the pre-caster to create a limited amount of components among pre-determined variety of product along with keep up architectural aesthetic importance. Furthermore, Open Building System is permitting hybrid submission along with flexible to standardization in addition to Modular Coordination based on CIDB, 2003a.

2.4.3 Modular Coordination

According to the classification recommended by Trikha in 1999, modular coordination is a synchronized incorporated system in favor of measurement spaces, mechanism, and decent. This enables all rudiments in shape together with no cutting or expanding even when the mechanism and fittings are contrived by dissimilar suppliers.

In 1999, Warszawski added that creating a basic modular coordination which is able to minimize various types of components and sizes that exist on it. By utilizing rationalized construction methods, each individual component is designed to be interchangeable with another similar so as to provide the maximum possible freedom to the designer. In addition, by recommending a desired size and limit the dimensions of building components and adopted the basic unit of measurement is relatively large base module can achieve the above objectives.

In the same year, i.e. in 1999 Warszawski also said that with more emphasis on the modular coordination will make it possible to facilitate the adoption of prefabricated components that are used for any layout as well as the ability to interchange them in the building. This can be achieved by defining the location of each component in the building with a modular grid leads to a general rather lead to the other components.

Coordination modular functional building component modules implement the basic unit of length M or equal to 100 cm, so for this size or the size of the increments can be applied to the production of building components by designers. Although this concept seems simple and easily adopted, but in the run involves a large degree of co-ordination as well as some adjustments in relation to aspects of the manufacturing process and interfacing components.

2.4.4 Standardization and Tolerances

All components need standards in its production in order to achieve the requirements of modular coordination. Standardization of spaces along with components compulsory situational acceptance at dissimilar stages of construction such as tolerance produced, set tolerances and tolerance of erections (Referring to Trikha 1999). This is to ensure that the united tolerances obtained on statistical reflections are within the limits permitted.

2.4.5 Mass Production

The venture in equipment, individual resources, and services that related with IBS is able to barely be well planned economical when there is huge amount of production. Such amount can supply a distribution of the unchanging investment allege over a outsized number of product items with no excessively mounting their ultimate cost based on CIDB Singapore in 1992.

2.4.6 Specialization

In 1999 Warszawski states that result in large-scale production and standardization of precast elements allows a high degree of labour specialization along the production process. To this it can be divided into a large number of small homogeneous tasks. In working condition created such workers are more open to their work which results in a higher level of productivity.

2.4.7 Good Organization

The volume of production is high, job specialization and concentrations of production requires an efficient organization and have experience (Warszawski 1999). A good organization must have a high level of planning, coordination and coordination and control functions related to the production and distribution of products IBS.

2.4.8 Integration, Planning and Control of the Processes

To get maximum results, Warszawski (1999) tells us that there must be a high degree of coordination among the various stakeholders such as manufacturing, designer and owner of the contractor. This is an archive through an integrated system in which all of these functions are carried out under the authority of a unified.

Assembly, design, manufacturing and other related processes requires a coherent structure and management from early to late in order to achieve desired goals and give their best to the customers. Thorough planning of all activities required especially in the early stages of design projects where activities require extra attention in the following aspects of architectural engineering, planning also preparatory.

Lessing et al in 1999 said that well equipped processes along with entire design when the production begins and the utilize of discretely extended technical system, sustained by prepared planning methods, the implementation of the process will scamper smooth along with a short amount of imperfection and errors. The strive is towards nil imperfection and minimum total of squander.

2.4.9 Production Facility

In 1986, Peng have shown that the onset of capital investment to build a plant that is permanent is dependent on experience. Workers are drawn; equipment, plant, and resource management needs to be obtained before production can actually begin. Investment can only be leveled if there is sufficient demand for the products of IBS. Viewed from another perspective, although casting yard or factory can be established at the project site to minimize transportation costs incurred.

2.4.10 Transportation

In 1986 Peng also said that casting large-panel system can minimize labor costs by as much as 30 percent. Unfortunately, the assumption of cost savings is countered by the cost of transportation. Transporting large panels also have to follow the requirements of the state road department. This is what you should consider when you want to use a prefabricated system.

2.4.11 Equipment at Site

For the reason of erecting along with assembling precast panels hooked on their situation, weighty crane is compulsory mainly for multi-story building. It is consequently essential to integrate this extra cost when accepting a prefabrication system.

2.5   The Advantage of IBS

Thanoon et al in 2003 has summarized advantages of IBS or industrialized building system when measure up to the conservative construction method as tag along:

a. a.   Prefabrication obtains place at a federal factory, therefore reducing effort requisite at site. Warszawski in 1999 confirmed that this is accurate particularly when far above the ground degree of mechanization occupied.

b. b.   In 1986, Peng gave a statement that IBS speed up construction time because they can simultaneously casting precast elements at work in the factory as well as the foundation's website. This of course can reduce construction time to a minimum as long as it has good coordination.

c. c.   Warszawski in 1999 said that IBS may permit suppleness in architectural design in order to reduce the monotony of recurring facades.

d. d.   Bing et al 2001 comment that the way to cut costs is simply by repeated use of system formwork made of steel, scaffolding, aluminum, etc.

a. e.   In the opinion of Peng in 1986, prefabricated components conducted in a controlled environment made construction operations are not affected by adverse weather conditions

b. f.   Zaini in 2000 said that the way to get our own unique method of construction is to create a different system using the IBS that gives flexibility in the design of precast elements in the development.

c. g.   Din in 1984 give the statement that IBS element is superior quality of elements all the way through careful selection of substances, use of highly developed technology along with better excellence control.

2.6   Shortcomings of IBS

The acceptance of IBS is not devoid of its limitations. Underneath discuss the deficiency of an IBS system.

a. a.   Trikha in 1999 recommended that an IBS system be able to merely be adequate to practitioners if its main beneficial can take over from the conventional system. Nevertheless up to date, there is insufficient corroborative methodical research undertaken to substantiate the benefits if IBS system. It is therefore, arguable that the accomplishment of IBS is mostly over-involved by be short of scientific information.

b. b.   A study conducted by Kampempool and Suntornpong in 1986 showed that the standardization of building elements face a lot of resistance from the construction industry to the reservation aesthetic reasons as well as economic reasons. One example that we should know that when a 300mm thick standard modular floor slab should be used despite the fact that the floor slab 260mm thick have similar structural performance. It's led to wastage of materials.

c. c.   Selection of new IBS experience many obstacles due to the lack of assessment criteria specified by the competent authority. Following the statement Trikha 1999, this phenomenon is more detrimental to the development of indigenous IBS. Given these problems, be deficient in of assessment criteria has been known as an inhibitor is most needed in the introduction of IBS system in this country.

d. d.   In an effort to introduce a modular coordination, since the 1980s Malaysia has done a very intensive marketing strategy, but unfortunately this is not getting a response that was so good in the building industry. It is directly delivered by Trikha in 1999. As a result of the poor response received, it makes the partial introduction of IBS such as stairs, lintels, etc. become possible.

e. e.   Warszawski IBS revealed that investment in the building industry to be much more at risk if we compare it with conventional methods of labor-intensive, it is because of the general decline of demand and market volatility for building large-scale public housing that exist in almost all developing countries. This statement is

21

quite reasonable because of the cheap imported labor spread across many European countries.

f.   f.   The process of industrialization development emphasis on the repetitiveness and standardization cause "barracklike" complex monotonous very often turn into severe slum area in a few years. In 1999 Warswaski tell that this shortcoming more evident in the presence of defects in the production of building components which are fairly common in the early stages of prefabricated. Damage is caused by the lack of expertise and poor quality control, causing aesthetic and functional errors, such as the penetration of moisture, stains, cracking and poor thermal insulation of the building when completed.

g.   g.   Warszawski in 1999 also emphasizes that the prefabricated components can be inflexible to changes that may be needed during his lifetime because it can happen when a small size range of prefabricated space used.

h.   h.   At the level of higher or university education, the introduction of students to technology, organization and design of IBS is lacking. Existing academic curriculum includes courses that combine rare overall potential, the procedures and methodology limitations associated with industrialization in development. As a consequence, Warszawski in 1999 suggests that there is a ordinary tendency surrounded by practitioners to prefer the conventional method potential by means of the intermittent utilize of a solitary prefabricated components.

i.   i.   Din in 1984 said that the joint standardization and connection details can inhibit the evolution of new technologies. The weak point of presented industrialized building system is tranquil in its unwieldy associations and jointing methods which are extremely responsive to inaccuracy and careless work.

a.   j.   An adaptation of standardization requires an effort of training and education seriously. Therefore, at the beginning of the investment requires considerable cost. Warsawski reveals that this is one of the biggest challenges in using modular coordination.

b.

2.7   IBS in another point of view

By using IBS it will reduce a large amount of labour both skilled and unskilled involved directly in that place. According to Warszawski in 1999, it has been demonstrated that a study conducted in Israel to perform a comparison between the conventional construction methods with IBS in 1984. The results of these studies indicate that the use of IBS has provided a lot of saving up as much 70persen and compared with conventional methods it is far save the total cost of construction. In line with those in Singapore, research conducted by Cheong in 1997 showed that the use of fully prefabricated system successfully deliver savings of up to as much as 46.5 percent when compared to conventional methods. This would decrease on the dependency of foreign labour workers. But somehow this does not affect the existing workforce in the country. The use of IBS will provide many opportunities to young people who looked hesitant to get involved in the construction industry.

Use of IBS can improve the professional labour force in Malaysia. One area that could be improved is the knowledge of the components of IBS. Development and research can be focused on areas to improve local industry so that dependence on foreign technology can be reduced as much as possible. Design created should give top priority to the climatic conditions, building traditions, materials and local social conditions. In 2006, Lim revealed that the design engineers, architects and contractors seeking economic solutions as closely as possible to the highest specification and speed of installation projects.

2003 Harwant et al give an idea of other solutions in the development of IBS can be started with a geology building materials and natural building materials. The need to use concrete and stone is not only material used in IBS. Building materials eligible to consider is a natural plaster, clay lightweight and monolithic adobe. The clay can be used as a wall light without pads while naturally as gypsum plaster, paint casein, lime and plaster the earth is a wise choice in the stage of completion of the surface of both interior and exterior walls. The monolithic adobe made of fireproof clay with straw as a binder for building walls. Use of this material is very helpful in the fight against dependence on concrete and masonry needs to be very helpful environmental conservation efforts. This is true especially when the construction is located in a remote area when the materials needed for construction is a problem.

At the time of IBS precision industrial manufacturing process is very important to learn so that they can meet the needs of the current locale in terms of cost savings, quality and speed. Increasing product variety without seriously affecting the production cost can be reached by standardizing the manufacturing process through modularization of components. In the implementation process of standardization of the manufacturing IBS have more chances to be accepted.

2.8   Experiences and Implementation of IBS in Other Countries

IBS has gained very wide popularity among a wide range of existing construction practitioners worldwide. The use of IBS in other countries is to implement legislative context into the local building regulations. Following the statement about the findings presented by Thanoon et al in 2003, IBS acceptance internationally proven to provide many benefits to every country who apply this system which have a positive impact on their construction sector. Here are some reviews on the use of IBS in some countries in the entire world.

2.8.1 Germany

The detailed investigation held by Glass in 1999, Germany is not too detailed regulations regarding secondary requirements that encourage the use of IBS to be more advantageous or economical than in the UK. Due to technological progress in German makes IBS market is very well established and competitive. The development is well recognized, especially precast internal and external walls along with precast roof panels. Therefore Thanoon in 2003 suggest that it is economical to set up a factory devoted exclusively to the assembly of precast concrete industry.

The German Building parameters are derived from representation parameters that are written primarily in convenient terms moreover issued through the Federal Government. Federal Building Code includes the regulation of development and planning laws so that building regulations include requirements that primarily serves to ensure the safety, public health and other matters regarding the design, site and building layout. Building codes are equipped with the technical regulations that serve to build products that differentiate among products that are non-regulatory and regulatory. Regulated products are usually the same as the technical regulations and conformity aiming for examination either by the manufacturer or a certificate of conformity certificate of conformity issued by an approved certification body. Suitability of non-regulated products were confirmed by in accordance with the universal technical agreement, a certificate of inspection along with endorsement or a special agreement for entity cases.

In Germany, the building control system activates throughout an arrangement submission, agreement along with inspection through local authority. Structural stability relies mostly on the suitable DIN Standards in favour of construction methods along with the supplies used in construction. In the meantime the fire shield standards are put out in DIN 4102 along with the echo insulation technical necessities are restricted in DIN 4019 that obliges the sound decrease of 53 dB in the barrier.

2.8.2 Netherlands

In Netherland, the using of IBS consists around 10 percent from the total housing market, even though the conventional masonry construction along with brick wall still succeed through the country. Nonetheless, following the examiner by Glass in 1999, the industrialized housing is gradually increasing because of the cost saving up till 30 percent. This is proved by standardized elements, better industrialized building technique and of course bendable manufacturing process.

Housing Act is the basis of building work in Netherland. The Incorporating Pronouncement which accompanied impact contains broadly uniform specialized enactment. The primary focuses are of the Building Pronouncement incorporates wellbeing, wellbeing and vitality economy, the execution of the building by reference to standard and important endorsements to congruity and Specialized Endorsement by producers as a verification of gathering the prerequisites. In any case, the city can't force separate specialized prerequisite on all the IBS components.

Open building idea was acquainted in Netherlands with take care of the popularity of mass lodging creation for its regular people. This idea has underscored on the application and use of IBS parts. As per Cuperus (1998), Open Building is a multi-facetted idea, with specialized, authoritative and money related answers for an assembled environment that can adjust to evolving needs. It underpins client support, industrialization and rebuilding of the building methodology.

The Building Decree is distributed as fourteen free sections covering the specialized regulations for development work and the condition of existing development meets expectations. It contains an accumulation of execution prerequisites, by which building arrangements can be tried utilizing estimations or computations and demonstrates, through a test worth, whether the necessities have been agreed to. The manufacturer can choose how to build and which materials to utilize giving the execution prerequisites are met. The Decree alludes to Dutch Standards concerning structures and structural designing works (Class A Standard). Procurement has been made in the Building Decree for Dutch Standards to be supplanted by blended European Standards as these get to be accessed.

More codes were presented from that point, and this denotes a development change in the building business in Netherlands. The building business is changing from expanding on location utilizing fundamental building materials to a get together process: complete and complex building parts are made in the production line and amassed on the site into a building.

Today, Netherlands is in the middle of one of the nation that leads in the submission of IBS parts in the development business. Its solid idea on the profits of Open Building which intends to advance the nature of the assembled environment, by enhancing the relationship between the client and the building business has pulled in numerous nations worldwide to look for the ability counsel from the Netherlands. The OBS has for sure helped to improve building along with development.

2.8.3 United Kingdom

The utilization of IBS in Britain got to be clearer in the mid-1900s after the boundless demolition of lodging units amid the Second World War. As indicated by Glass (1999), in excess of 165,000 precast solid homes had been fabricated going from little single lodge to expansive tall structures by 1960.

In 1999, the precast solid speaks to around 25 percent of the business sector for cementations items. This incorporates an extensive variety of items utilized as a part of the development business, for example, suspended floors, structural squares, clearing, cast stone and engineering cladding of these items, the suspended floors speak to the higher utilization with yield in term of tones of item sold for every annum.

Regulation 9 instructs that the necessities of the regulations can be fulfilled just by agreeability with the significant models. The significant models are situated out in this record, the Technical Standards for agreeability with the Building Standards Regulations 1990, as revised. To fulfill the regulations accordingly the outline, materials and routines for development must be in any event to the benchmarks set in the specialized standard. The procurements esteemed to fulfill the gauges are accommodated the comfort of fashioners just on the off chance that they decide to receive them. There is no commitment to do so yet in the event that utilized legitimately esteemed to fulfill arrangements must be acknowledged by the neighborhood power.

In the specialized standard in the Building Standard 1990, in the Chapter 9 Part G2.6 sub C said that the suspended carpet utilizing IBS components need to give protection over the boards. The nonbearing pre-assembled dividers are obliged to take after the BS 8297: 1995. The BS 476 determined the blaze test and necessities for structures and BS 8297: 1995 is the code of practice for outline and establishment of non-load bearing precast solid divider cladding.

In BS 6750: 1986 indicates necessity for particular reference framework, positions of key references planes and the estimating of the building and their parts and material planned in agreeability of standards of secluded coordination. It likewise tagged the particular matrices, positions of measured floor plane, secluded stature and the measured space. The outline details, joints and fits and the dimensioning are institutionalized. Then again, BS EN ISO: 1999 are the institutionalization of the development drawings which control in the representation of secluded sizes, lines and matrices. With this gauges accessible, it is simpler for the planner and fabricator to institutionalize regarding sizes, drawings and the idea.

IBS has assumed a tremendous part in the development business in Britain. Later on, it is normal that IBS segments will assume control over the traditional workmanship development that has hoard the business sector for quite a while as of now.

2.8.4 United States of America

IBS has started as ahead of schedule as the 1930s as seen by the development of pre-assembled steel houses by General Homes in those days. Nonetheless, because of cost in aggressiveness, high capital speculation and conflicting nearby codes, the early dream to promote IBS as an imaginative development technique started to blur off. On the other hand, after the Second World War, the pattern was raised again because of the climbing need to resolution the basic lack of houses.

As per Glass (1999), a study was done via Portland Cement Association (PCA) showed that 70 percent of purchasers in the US market select their fantasy house on the premise of expense/esteem alone. As such, the focal points regarding structural completions, adaptability and great warm protection were seen as an auxiliary concern just. Notwithstanding, the mentality of purchasers have in the end changed and purchasers to look into of rate and simplicity of development, and above all, the nature of final item when acquiring a house, in this manner settling on IBS as a prevalent decision of strategy for development.

In the condition of Georgia, there are a few codes that are seen to guarantee the consistency in the development of industrialized building. The distinctive areas of the Codes detail diverse materials, technique for development or different necessities and in this way the most prohibitive standard will oversee. On the off chance that there are contention between general necessity and particular prerequisite and the recent might be appropriate. Interchange materials and development strategy can be utilized yet it needs the approbation from the Commissioner gave the reason planned meet the determinations in the specialized codes.

In the Georgia Standard Building Code, the regulations incorporates the details weight of building material for transportation and the base roof stature should be 7 feet (2181mm). The nearby power of the state has the ability to represent over the creator, producer and the constructor. The creator is legislated through the accommodation of arrangement though the producer need to submit the quality control manual for support before the development can be initiated. The nature of the constructor establishment of pre-assembled is administered by the agent from the nearby power.

In the United States of America, timber encircled is for the most part utilized for low climb lodging, while cement precast framework is constantly utilized seriously especially as a part of territory that are powerless against ecological risks thusly sea tempests and tornadoes. Cement precast framework is additionally connected in the development of tall structure in the USA because of its speed and simplicity in development.

With the setting up of BAIHP or The Building America Industrialized Housing Partnership, more explores and discoveries are completed seriously to plan the best engineering and development strategies to further advance IBS in USA. Through such association, IBS is picking up quick notoriety in the USA advertise regarding skyscraper and low climb structures.

2.8.5 Japan

As indicated by Nagahama (2000), the industrialization of lodging industry in Japan began in 1960s and from that point forward, the piece of the pie has changed drastically with the utilization and application of IBS.

As reported, from April 1999 to March 2000, development of pre-assembled houses in Japan spoke to 20 percent of all houses implicit Japan amid that period. Out of that, the steel confining framework commanded the pre-assembled business sector with a 73 percent offer, took after next by the application of wood encircling which remains at 18 percent, while the strengthened solid surrounding just accounted 9 percent of the pre-assembled business sector.

With reference to this, the wood-confined lodging developed 2 percent and steel lodging developed 3 percent, while cement encircled lodging accomplished a significant setback of 12 percent. Despite that, the Japan development industry is still viewed as profoundly coordinated and computerized generation supplies and offices to fabricate house building parts and offers home purchasers both quality and stylish dream house.

2.8.6 Singapore

The need to finish substantial amounts of lofts in the early 60s for dire lodging needs as fast as could be allowed has provoked The Housing and Development Board (HDB) of Singapore to receive the IBS system. The accentuation then was less on style. By the mid-70s, the lodging circumstance had enhanced and more consideration required to be given to give an aggregate living environment to inhabitants. At this stage, the prerequisite for feel and completing quality started to develop. This pattern carried on to the 80s and in the 90s, seeing new ideas like mass customization rising.

In view of the report by Tat and Hao (1999), amid the period from 19731979, HDB of Singapore has again took a daring activity to endeavor IBS in perspective of the requirement for finishing 100,000 abode units of lodging units. As an aftereffect of constant exertion, the HDB has made a striking accomplishment in the selection of IBS for the development of people in general lodging system. These activities are the fuse of measured co-appointment of its open lodging outlines, outline institutionalization and customization, construction, and the automation of site operations.

The setting up of HDB Prefabrication Technology Centre (PTC) in 1994 imprints an alternate development accomplishment in the application of IBS in Singapore. Ptc's primary exercises are to outline, create and produce pre-assembled building items; behaviour innovative work of cutting edge and inventive development materials and frameworks; oversee and supply pre-assembled building items; behaviour preparing and permit its licensed innovation rights.

The application of IBS in the development business in Singapore is picking up high notoriety because of its numerous profits. Through its own particular exploration Centre, HDB has presented significant development in the territory of IBS parts, all things considered precast reject chute, precast Ferro concrete auxiliary top boards, precast volumetric family shield, precast section, precast exterior, and precast parapet et cetera. Figure 2.9 show illustrations of creative IBS segments created in Singapore.

2.8.7 Thailand

The utilization of IBS as an inventive development strategy in Thailand has got higher fame than the situation development industry in Thailand in 1970 back. As indicated by an announcement Buddhi unveiled in 2004, the Thai government has arrangements to fabricate around 600,000 units were begun in 2004 for a long time for individuals with centre to lower earnings. The majority of the family units are withdrawn.

Appointed designers and creators have proposed distinctive lodging frameworks. Nonetheless, it is paramount to note that as far as material, creation and development, the configuration must be suitable for extensive scale development inside a constrained time and expense. In July 2004, the NHA or National Housing Authority of Thailand has

Figure 2. 9 Examples of innovative IBS components produced in Singapore

Approved the usage of the PLPC or Precast Large Panel Construction. This imprints an alternate turning point for the development business in Thailand, where a few thousand PLPC houses will be assembled inside a time of a few years.

PLPC is an alternate illustration of IBS parts broadly utilized as a part of Thailand. PLPC structural framework comprises of typically strengthened precast solid boards, precast pieces and establishments. No shaft and sections are utilized aside from a few areas. Regarding the velocity of development, the aggregate time needed is essentially short of what the customary framework. As indicated by Buddhi (2004), for an ordinary 2-3 room two story house, the

31

time needed for throwing, lifting, erection and finishing of structural framework is around 2-4 days once the framework is setup. This shows how quick a normal house based focused around IBS idea can reach, as contrasted with ordinary development system. Figure 2.10 demonstrate the application of PLPC in the development business in Thailand.

Different favourable circumstances of utilizing PLPC, which incorporates large scale manufacture, no evacuation of formwork, less or practically identical structural expense, quality control, use of talented work, low beginning speculation, modularization and mechanization and solidness and long haul execution. Thailand is one of the nation's eagerly bringing IBS development strategy into its development industry. It is anticipated that the Government of Thailand will have the capacity to attain its focus in giving 600,000 units of lodging units to its low and medium wage bunch, therefore giving the essential necessities to its regular folks, much appreciated Figure 2.10: The application of PLPC in development industry of Thailand

2.8.8 Denmark

Figure 2. 10 Example of PLPC in Denmark

As indicated by Gibbons (1986), in Denmark, around 80 percent of the confined houses delivered since the mid-1960 was utilizing IBS, the greater part of it penalized framework. The IBS application in Denmark is gone for local and fare markets. For example, its global foremen, for example, Jespersen & Son and Larsen & Nielsen have developed a lot of people extensive scale ventures all

Through the world, utilizing pre-assembled solid framework created from the nearby industrial facilities in their nation.

In short, Denmark is not exceptionally lingering behind regarding progression in the application of IBS in its development industry. The development organizations from the nation are eagerly advancing IBS parts from their nation to the outside world.

2.8.9 History of IBS in Malaysia

The activity to utilize and present IBS as a part of Malaysia began off back in the early sixties, when the Minister of Housing and Local Government went to some European nations and assessed their building frameworks execution. Noise (1984) reported that, it was then that the two pilot activities utilizing IBS idea was completed in 1964 where the first pilot undertaking was 7 pieces of 17 story pads and 4 squares of 4 story pads which involve 3000 units of minimal effort pads and 40 units of shop parcels in Kuala Lumpur. The undertaking actualized huge board framework utilizing the Danish System with IBS idea of development.

The second pilot venture was inherent Penang, with the development of 6 squares of 17 story pads and 3 pieces of 18 story pads, involving 3,699 units and 66 shop parts, utilizing French Estiot System. With reference to the two pilot ventures, it is figured out that as far as examination of execution between IBS framework and routine framework focused around expense, gainfulness and quality component, the general execution of IBS is more aggressive than the traditional technique.

Since 1980"s there are concentrated showcasing method dispatched by the Malaysian government to present particular coordination, Trikha (1999) reported that its acknowledgement has gotten poor reactions for the building business. Thus even incomplete presentation of IBS, for example, lintels and staircase has not been conceivable.

At one time in the seventh Malaysian Plan, the nation planned to develop around 800,000 units of houses for its populace utilizing the IBS development. To be sure, 585,000 units were anticipated the low and low medium expense houses. However the accomplishments are baffling with just 20 percent finished houses reported because of utilization of routine development system. As indicated by Ismail (2001), in spite of the fact that the legislature acquainted various motivations and advancements with sway lodging designers to put resources into such lodging class, the reaction is not all that positive. Under the seventh Malaysian Plan, the requirement of Modular Coordination through the Construction Industry Standard 1 and 2 just applies to the minimal effort lodging tasks started by the Ministry of

Housing and Local Government Malaysia (CIDB 2003a). The authorization by the nearby powers did not make a difference to all the gatherings included in the development help the disappointment of the usage in Malaysia. Moreover, the impetuses that guaranteed to be given to designers by the legislature does not plainly expressed in the law of Malaysia. This non-conformance prompts the use customary system which is less dangerous to the designers.

In 1998, the Ministry of Housing and Local Government and CIDB has thought of the Modular Design Guide which contain the measured coordination ideas, outline administers, drawings and favoured measurements for design completes material, for example, blocks, glass, gypsum board and so forth. The imperative parts of pre-assembled solid as far as measured measurements, quality, soundness and the blaze assurance details are not demonstrated. The Uniform Building By Law (UBBL) has acquainted a few conditions with energize the utilization of IBS incorporate the sub condition of 42(1):

a. The second line of the statement said that „11 meter square horrible area" is supplanting the 10.8 meter square net area. This is suitable for the territory of room that has the measurement of 3000mm x 3600mm and utilizing the secluded measurement.
b. The fourth line of the proviso expressed that 9.3 meter square terrible area" is supplanting the 9.0 meter square net area".
c. The fifth line of the proviso specified that 6.5 meter square terrible area is supplanting by 6.3 meter square net area.

In the routine development extend the neighbourhood power just given to investigate the work after the fulfilment of the task. The legislature ought to investigate permitting the nearby power to examine the work in the assembling process up to the development stage and in conclusion to the undertaking finish to guarantee that quality is not bargained.

In year 2001, the Government set the Malaysia Standard 1064 so as to institutionalize the IBS segments as far as measurements. However the MS 1064 still have a considerable measure of provisos that still can be moved forward. The vital particulars, for example, sorts of material, configuration standard, association sorts, development strategy and the framework execution are excluded. These things will guarantee the nature of IBS segments can be enhanced and the foreman can actualize an institutionalized framework effortlessly and this will empower the utilization of IBS in Malaysia particularly in the private part. However the principles should not be excessively unbending as to take into consideration mechanical changes in development system, framework and so forth.

As indicated by discoveries of Lim (2006), numerous advancements in materials and parts are made before their application in the building procedure. As a rule, development firm goes about as framework integrators and impetus for changing new advances into attractive items. These assume a paramount part changing and creating new innovations that effect as criticism circle to makers in the upstream. The strengths for engineering for adjustment are strongest among materials, part makers and fantastic supplies for creation purposes. Property designers and government strategy producers likewise sustain the stream for development by financing in.

2.9   Impediments to Progress of IBS in Malaysia

The legislature as the significant key player in the development business has used billions of Ringgit over the past a few Malaysia Plans to create the nation. However, the arrangements are portrayed by deficiencies, postpones and absence of coordination between all gatherings including the organizations at government and state levels and other real players in the development business. Salihuddin (2003) remarked that the legislature has not taken vital activities for the globalization and the industrialization of the development business. Then, Trikha (1999) included that the determination of IBS has been blocked by the absence of evaluation criteria set by the affirming powers.

An IBS framework must be rehearsed by the professional in the event that its real focal points are significant contrasted with the ordinary framework. However forward, there is deficient community investigative examination attempted to substantiate the profits of IBS framework. Thusly it can be plainly seen that the execution of IBS is obstructed by absence of investigative data as remarked by Razali et al (2002). Warszawski (1999) accentuated that the scholastic educational module in the college sometimes fuse courses that engineering,

35

association, development and the configuration of IBS. Regardless Thanoon (2003) specified that absence of innovative work to utilize the neighbourhood materials causes the reliance of remote engineering can be extravagant and the nature of items may be traded off.

The divided development industry straddles over a few callings and business. Salihuddin (2003) pointed out that the experts, manufacturers and the supplier don't convey to enter on thoughts on usage of IBS. However the fundamental attentiveness toward these gatherings are simply benefit and the imperviousness to change because of vague motivators given by the legislature by utilizing new innovation.

The examination yield from exploration establishment is not promptly economically exploitable and does not speak to potential clients. The significant players of the development business are hesitant to do the innovative work in IBS on the grounds that this can be seen as dangerous wanders. The nation has not been left upon strategic investing in a proactive serious way and in that capacity exertion in colleges and examination establishments remain generally unexploited and unused.

All gatherings included in the development business ought to work together and to cooperate keeping in mind the end goal to attain the full usage of IBS in Malaysia. The administration assumes a vital part in forcing new regulations, norms and preparing regarding learning, background and development technique. In addition the institutionalization of measurements of material needs to give a criticism circle from the constructor to empower the execution to be enhanced occasionally. Motivating forces given by government ought to be plainly reported and verifying that all gatherings is decently educated through advancements by the media. To wrap things up, the administration ought to host the power over gatherings included including producer, constructor, planner, budgetary foundation and the transporters to guarantee they assume their individual parts in the effective execution of IBS.

2.9.1 Development of IBS in Malaysia

As per Badir et al. (2002), there are no less than 21 suppliers and makers heartily included in advancing IBS in Malaysia. Be that as it may, greater parts of the IBS parts are begun from the United States, Germany and Australia, though Malaysia just helped a more modest share of created IBS segments.

This demonstrates that there are still plentiful of spaces for development and subsequently advancing the application of IBS as a creative development system in our nation is still broadly open. Figure 2.11 demonstrates the wellsprings of IBS in Malaysia as per the beginning of nations.

As per Budget (2004), Former Finance Minister, YAB Dato" Seri Abdullah Ahmad Badawi on 10 September 2004 amid the Budget 2005 publication, has empowered the use of IBS segments in Government building undertakings and would be expanded from 30 percent to 50 percent initiating 2005. Lodging designers, who use IBS segments surpassing 50 percent, will be given full exception on toll forced by CIDB. This demonstrates that the Government is attempting to empower the utilization of IBS parts in the development ventures in our nation.

As indicated by CIDB (2003), just 15 percent of the nearby development industry has utilized IBS as a part of Malaysia. In any case, regardless of the high introductory venture expense, a few engineers in Malaysia with sufficient economies of scale have made proactive strides and put resources into IBS, chiefly in formwork and structure. As indicated by these designers, IBS gave better and steadier quality to their structures, better site administration with less reliance on outside laborers.

As indicated by Malaysian Industry-Government Group for High Technology MIGHT (2003) amid a gathering on 24 January 2003 led by Datuk Eddy Chen, REHDA Immediate Past Present, it is recognized that:

IBS has been honed to a certain degree in Malaysia. PKNS, for example, have fabricated in excess of 25,000 lodging units utilizing industrialized frameworks. JKR likewise reported that they are utilizing IBS for government quarters being developed all over Malaysia

In Jkrs's case, they outline the segments (prefab chunks, shafts, sections, infill boards) and focused around the details, the business concocts made items. Their outlines are such that they can either do secluded and IBS, or ordinary.

There are no short of what 70 frameworks accessible in the business sector. As being what is indicated, there is a need to really concur on a definition on IBS. With a fitting definition, the following game plan is to get acknowledgement from powers, money related foundations, and so on.

That IBS ought to be identified with skyscraper, as well as low climb advancements furthermore business structures.

Secluded coordination (MC) must be accentuated. Information of MC at all levels (counting nearby authorities" staff) must be improved. Everyone, from holder to architect to powers and foremen must acquaint themselves with MC to avert event of gigantic mold alterations for each new activities – which is expense ineffectual.

From consultants" perspective – at present they need to do 2 outlines (routine and industrialized) on the grounds that defining the plans as industrialized will bring about the customer getting little number of tenderers amid tendering procedure.

Concurred that there ought to be components of incentivization to IBS clients – designers, experts and so forth. Motivating forces ought to additionally be given for fractional IBS use.

Whether our human asset is prepared to embrace IBS.
In spite of the fact that the CIDB has drawn up the IBS Roadmap, Modular Design Guide, indexes of pre-assembled segments and numerous different aides with some reference to usage objectives and courses of events, accomplishments to date are indistinct and of little effect. Towards this end, it is fundamental for CIDB to captivate specialists with fitting

specialized aptitudes to attempt a top to bottom study on what is obliged to create and advance IBS, including an expansive expense advantage investigation, points of interest on the execution plan with clear breakthroughs and deliverables.

The Government ought to set time span to slowly decrease admission of remote work into the development business. A checking component will likewise need to be set up to track advancement of IBS industry improvement with destination key execution pointers (Kpis). Vellu (2004) was cited as saying; "effective execution of the movement to IBS is required to help the legislature in reaching its focus of diminishing outside work reliance by 85 percent".

For this framework to be effectively used, both open and private segments would need to assume their parts in instructing the neighbourhood development industry. Be that as it may aside from wilfully evolving attitude, there must be some push variable to catalyse the shift in outlook. Maybe a decent combo of carrot and stick, i.e. motivators and administrative necessities for the presentation and selection of IBS ought to be the following cement arrangement of activity to be initiated by CIDB to further advance IBS in the development business in our nation.

Today, the utilization of IBS as a strategy for development in Malaysia is advancing. Numerous privately owned businesses in Malaysia have collaborated with outside master from Australia, Netherlands, United State and Japan to offer precast answer for their task (CIDB, 2003b). What's more, more nearby makers have made themselves in the business sector. Precast, steel casing and different IBS were utilized as cross breed development to construct national point of interest, for example, Bukit Jalil Sport Complex, Lightweight Railway Train (LRT) and Petronas Twin Tower. It was accounted for in the examination of Thanoon (2003) that no less than 21 of different producers and suppliers of IBS are eagerly advancing their framework in Malaysia. All things considered, the administration of Malaysia still feels that the utilization of IBS is still low regardless of the conceivable potential. From the overview directed by CIDB of Malaysia in 2003, the utilization level of IBS in nearby development industry remains at 15 percent (CIDB, 2003b). The aggregate enlisted IBS builders in Malaysia stand for 1,993 in year 2007 as indicated in Table 2.2 and Table 2.3 and enrolled IBS maker in Malaysia until 2007 is 138, which delivering 347 IBS items accessible in the business sector as demonstrated in Table 2.4.

Apparently that a large portion of mainly created items are focused around conventional materials, for example, strengthened solid and the most creative materials are focused around foreign made engineering (CIDB, 2007b). There is no required prerequisite on any affirmation or accreditation of parts, organizations or installers set up. Whilst, there is no exact information, there is some recounted proof recommends that there has been sporadic dumping of sub-standard remote items in Malaysia (CIDB, 2007b). A component to guarantee IBS items stamped to a worthy standard must be presented in the assembling methodology. Testing of parts, confirm and affirm them would restrict just protected and worthy IBS boards are raised and in this way CIDB will lead.

Table 2. 2 Enlisted IBS Contractor (Active) in Malaysia by IBS Grade (B01, B02, B12, B15 and B19 (2007), Source: CIDB Malaysia (Zuhairi, 2008)

GRADE	SPECIALTIES	TOTAL
B 01	Buildings and Industrial Pre-casting Work	28
B 02	Buildings and Industrial Steel Structure Work	516
B 12	Aluminium, Glass and Steel Work	232
B 15	Roofing and Steel Cladding Works	108
B 19	Special Framework	11
	GRAND TOTAL	895

Table 2. 3 Registered IBS Contractor (Active) in Malaysia by CIDB Grade (2007), Source: CIDB Malaysia (Zuhairi, 2008)

GRADE	NUMBER
G7	334
G6	52
G5	83
G4	42
G3	191
G2	76
G1	71
TOTAL	849

Table 2. 4 Registered IBS Manufacturer and IBS Products available in Malaysia, Source: Suruhanjaya Syarikat Malaysia (SSM) (Zuhairi, 2008)

MATERIAL	MANUFACTURER	PRODUCT	LOCAL	FOREIGN
PC Panel, Frame, Box	51	245	27	3
Steel				
Frames/Panel Components	30	45	16	1
Systems Formwork	29	29	14	3
Timber Frames	28	28	13	2
TOTAL	138	347	70	9

2.10 IBS Roadmap 2003 -2010

CIDB has distributed IBS Roadmap 2003-2010 which involved the needs and prerequisite of Malaysian development industry. This guide was embraced by bureau on 29th October 2003. The Roadmap is a complete archive that separated the IBS program into the five primary centre territories as indicated in Figure 2.12 that reflect the inputs required to drive the system, each one starting with M. They are Manpower, Materials, Management, Monetary, and Marketing (CIDB, 2003). The inputs are then partitioned into its components and the exercises to be executed for every component were then distinguished and included into the time compass of the Roadmap keeping in mind the end goal to accomplish the mission inside the stipulated timeline. Around 109 turning points are situated to be accomplished in year 2010. The substance of this Roadmap is cantered towards accomplishing the industrialization of the development part and the more drawn out term destination heading towards Open Building Systems idea.

As per IBS Roadmap 2003-2010, the key components of the guide are as per the following:

1. 1. To have a work arrangement that step by step decreases rate of remote specialists from the current 75 percent to 55 percent in 2005, 25 percent in 2007 and 15 percent in 2009,

2. 2. To join IBS/MC in expert courses for engineers, designers and others,

3. 3. To fuse syllabus on IBS/MC in structural engineering, designing, building courses in nearby colleges,

4. 4. To uphold Modular Coordination (MC) by neighbourhood powers through Uniform Building by Law (UBBL),

5. 5. To create list of building segments and standard arrangements for lodging

6. 6. To create IBS Verification plan,

7. 7. To implement use of IBS for 30 percent of aggregate government task (building) in 2004 and step by step expanding to 50 percent in 2006 and 70 percent in 2008,

8. 8. To present constructability program for all private building and authorization from 2008, and

9. 9. To give charge impetuses to producer of IBS segments

10. 10.   To offer green path program, for clients of standard arrangements (planned utilizing standard IBS Components and MC), and

11. 11.   To begin seller creating program, preparing and budgetary support.

Figure 2. 11 IBS 5M Component Elements (IBS Roadmap 2003)

As such, it is imperative to research fraternity and construction industry stakeholders to collaborate and ensure that any research project is not only able to create new knowledge but must also be aware of the requirements needed to bring the idea to the market and apply. In order to formulate the R&D for IBS strategy, CREAM has organized workshops, seminars and dialogue with the industry players from 2006 and 2007. This document is based from the outcome of the workshops and discusses.

CREAM"s strategic direction address long term requirement for R&D on IBS for the Malaysian construction industry.

One of the important milestones in the roadmap is the introduction of Modular Coordination (MC) concept. The system allows standardization in design and building components (CIMP, 2006-2015). It will encourage participation from manufactures and assemblers to enter the market, thus reducing the price of IBS components. In essence, MC will facilitate open industrialization which is the prime target of the roadmaps. The proposed enforcement of using MC through Uniform Building By-Law (UBBL) would encourage the adoption through standardization and the use of IBS components. However, until the end of 2007, the UBBL have yet to be amended to include MC regulations (Zuhairi *et al,* 2008).

Another important step taken by the government of Malaysia is to introduce incentives for IBS adopter. The exemption of the CIDB levy in 0.125 percent of total cost of the project according to Article 520 on contractors that implanted some kind of IBS in at least 50 percent of the building components was introduced effectively from 1st January 2007. In the first half of 2007, there were only 24 residential projects qualified for the levy exemption. It is a very small percentage of total 417 residential projects during that period (Zuhairi *et al,* 2008). It shows that awareness among developers and contractors on the levy exemption is still very low.

IBS Centre established in 2006 at Jalan Chan Sow Lin, Cheras, Kuala Lumpur will be one-stop Centre of IBS related programs initiated by CIDB, provide the training and consultancy on IBS and showcase IBS technology through the demonstration As being what is indicated, it is basic to research clique and development industry stakeholders to work together and guarantee that any examination undertaking is ready to make new learning as well as be mindful of the prerequisites required to bring the thought to the business and apply. To detail the R&d for IBS technique, CREAM has composed workshops, classes and dialog with the business players from 2006 and 2007. This archive is based from the result of the workshops and examines.

Cream's key bearing that address long haul prerequisite for R&d on IBS for the Malaysian development industry.

One of the critical breakthroughs in the guide is the presentation of Modular Coordination (MC) idea. The framework permits institutionalization in outline and building segments (CIMP, 2006-2015). It will energize support from fabricates and constructing agents to enter the business sector, in this way decreasing the cost of IBS segments. Basically, MC will encourage open industrialization which is the prime focus of the guides. The proposed implementation of utilizing MC through Uniform Building By-Law (UBBL) would support the reception through institutionalization and the utilization of IBS parts. Notwithstanding, until the end of 2007, the UBBL have yet to be revised to incorporate MC regulations (Zuhairi et al, 2008).

An alternate imperative step taken by the administration of Malaysia is to present motivations for IBS adopter. The absolution of the CIDB require in 0.125 percent of aggregate expense of the venture as indicated by Article 520 on builders that embedded an IBS in no less than 50 percent of the building parts was presented viably from first January 2007. In the first a large portion of 2007, there were just 24 private undertakings fit the bill for the duty exception. It is a little rate of aggregate 417 private undertakings amid that period (Zuhairi et al, 2008). It demonstrates that mindfulness among engineers and builders on the toll exception is still low.

IBS Centre created in 2006 at Jalan Chan Sow Lin, Cheras, Kuala Lumpur will be one-stop Centre of IBS related projects started by CIDB, give the preparation and consultancy on IBS and showcase IBS engineering through the showing venture. The commitment to actualize IBS systems and exercises from this Centre serves simultaneous both to enhance execution and quality in development, additionally to minimize the reliance of untalented outside work's flooding the development mark project. The obligation to implement IBS strategies and activities from this Centre serves concurrent both to improve performance and quality in construction, also to minimize the dependency of unskilled foreign labour's flooding the construction market.

2.10.1 IBS Roadmap Mid-Term Report

The IBS Centre has arranged however not yet distributed IBS Roadmap Mid-term report to study the current status of IBS selection in Malaysia on October 2007. The report has highlighted the worries that were adjusted from paper distributed by Construction Research Institute of Malaysia (CREAM) via Zuhairi et al (2008).

The report highlighted that skyscraper improvement and „factory-like" building have a tendency to have higher reception of IBS than arrived properties and little business units. At presents, basic practice shows assembling of IBS parts are included just after delicate phase of the worth chain. IBS need to be tended to in the configuration stage to be effective embraced.

As per Zuhairi (2008), whilst there is no exact information, there is some narrative confirmation, recommend that there has been sporadic dumping of sub-standard outside IBS item in IBS. A system to guarantee IBS items stamped to a satisfactory standard must be presented in the assembling methodology. There is yet any certificate or accreditation of segments organizations and installers set up. Littler builders view IBS as dangers and not as circumstances. There is absence of coordinated activity plan to execute the IBS Roadmap 2003-2010.

It appears that most mainly created items focused around customary materials, for example, strengthened solid and that most utilizing imaginative materials are focused around foreign made innovation. Until year 2007, seller improvement project have not yet been performed. The confirmation of item and installers has yet to be executed until the year of 2007.

The reception of IBS in Malaysia is simply customer driven. The builder just utilize IBS as option alternative, either expressly or through difficult time and quality necessities, requested by customers. Out of 109 IBS Roadmap developments, just 54 breakthroughs have been accomplished until year 2007.

2.11 Barriers to the Implementation of IBS

Unmistakably, the profits offered by IBS are massive and conceivable. It has been six years since the starting of the IBS Roadmap 2003 and is about the end of the mission of industrializing development. The development business' stakeholders are smidgen distrustful on utilizing IBS item. It is apropos to analyse the advancement and how near the finish of the mission to date. All the more essentially, it is basic to assess whether the execution of the guide has met the business reaction to the IBS program in this way. Most strategy issues have been determined and actualized, while all pertinent archives needed to help the project, have been produced. Specifically exercises under the charge of CIDB are all gathering their datelines. Despite these accomplishments various usage obstacles were distinguished as being potential obstacles to the execution of the guide.

Warszawski (1999) pointed out a portion of the obstructions in executing industrialization in development industry. There are decrease popular and unstable of building business make an interest in IBS more unsafe contrasted with ordinary work serious strategy. Construction components are viewed as rigid concerning changes with may require over its life compass. At college level understudy are less presented to engineering, association and configuration of industrialized building framework. An adjustment of institutionalization obliges a colossal instruction and preparing exertion. Institutionalization of building components face safety from development industry because of style reservation and financial reasons (Kampempool

46

et al, 1986).

Trikha (1999) referred to the obstruction to the utilization of IBS because of absence of evaluation criteria set by the affirming powers to urge the designers to utilize IBS. Poor reaction from the development players to secluded coordination in spite of overwhelming advancements and impetuses from the administration is additionally an obstruction to the progressive execution of IBS in Malaysia. Thus, incomplete presentation of IBS, for example, lintels and staircase has not been fruitful represent a viable rival to the conventional cast in situ outline.

In the mean time, Lim (2006) additionally highlighted ICT issues, which are concern with the information and data accessible to the framework, clients, customers, foundation of assembling design and methodology, and allotment of assets and materials. Transportation of boards and modules is a great deal more troublesome than transporting the total of their part. A 20 percent harm rate is not unordinary amid the first couple of years in IBS venture.

Thanoon ET. al. (2003) likewise highlighted shabby work expense is the fundamental boundaries to the undertaking of IBS. There are wide swing in house requests, though primarily brought on by the high investment rate and low execution in sparing component. He likewise brought up absence of talented development workforce which serious the circumstances. The nature qualities of development task which are divided, assorted and include numerous gatherings. Their absence of nearby R&d and novel building framework that utilize neighbourhood material, which makes IBS regularly depends to foreign made innovation from different nations. There are additionally inadequate impetus and advancement from the legislature to utilize IBS.

Reasonability of IBS rely on upon numerous elements; plan, standard, volume and consistency (Payne, 1977). The administration of Malaysia still feels that the use of IBS is still low regardless of the conceivable potential. From the study led by CIDB.

Malaysia in 2003, the use level of IBS in neighbourhood development industry remains at 15 percent (CIDB, 2003b). Zuihairi et al (2008) reported that the majority of by regional standards created items are focused around conventional materials, for example, strengthened solid and the most imaginative materials are focused around transported in engineering. There is no required necessity on any accreditation or accreditation of segments, organizations or installers set up.

Rahman et al (2006) pointed out the impediments in IBS execution, which reflected that the vehicle and joining inclination can't overcome lacking in volume, settled cost of device and structure can push unit cost up if investment is needing, which oftentimes is the circumstances of nonappearance of open region help. If considered the additional organization and arrangements cost, the total whole of stores by grasping IBS would be short of what 10 percent. Foundation of heavier and more personality boggling sections would further raise the capital costs, volume necessities and powerlessness.

IBS can't save the general work cost by utilizing more lighter-weight part, which warrants more work cost. Any reported greater saving was not on account of augmentation of viability of IBS, yet primarily as a result of diminishment of worth or to use less land, where this is not the certified point of IBS. Low work cost of the mud piece industry using straightforward system and awkward work has made work genuine procedures prepared to battle viably with an era process.

More bona fide is the issue of making joints, locking, staying, welding, beating or snapping parts together which need time and experience for perfection and diminished wastage. Execution of stunning sections is routinely adjusted by patchwork or poor fits and by right on time parts. Likewise, the technique itself including mechanized system and capable worker presents enthusiasm of precision not needed in other framework. A country can't remained to build immense volume of staying or close the cabin deficiency fast paying little admiration to productive if these are to be developed with remote made structure and cranes. Rate of improvement changed over to cash related saving is little.

Rahman et al (2006) further added to the rundown of difficulties to embrace IBS in Malaysian development industry is that the term IBS is frequently misconstrued with negative importance connected with 1960''s mechanical building. These building are ordinarily connected with low nature of building and obnoxious structural engineering appearance. The business is absence of information and presentation to IBS innovation and outline. There is absence of neighbourhood configuration practical of IBS framework in the business sector to satisfy the prerequisites. This has something to manage the absence of general mindfulness among development players themselves

.

Hussein (2007) additionally highlighted the hindrances in usage of IBS are chiefly the mentality issue towards attaining acknowledgement by the development group. The expenses of utilizing IBS surpass the ordinary strategy for development given the simplicity of securing modest foreigner work. IBS outline idea is not being mulled over at the onset of the undertaking Designers won't plan utilizing parts as they not find the segments in the business, whilst makers won't create parts as they don't see configuration utilizing parts .He additionally brought up that there are apathetic acknowledgement of IBS among originators and designers particularly from private divisions.

Lim (2006) expressed the accompanying deficiency in his examination to IBS execution in Malaysia. He additionally called attention to the structure of development industry is viewed as divided where the entire production network get their technique and motivation. The issues confronted by the development business are additionally because of conflict of arrangement rule usage and backing from the legislature.

The business is uncompetitive because of absence of open cooperation. Foremen in Malaysia are committing to close framework and getting supply from the same produce all through the development. IBS need large scale manufacture to attain monetary feasibility. Nonetheless, in Malaysia there is no affirmation of progression in the generation of segments. Nearby powers are unrealistic to roll out improvement in neighbourhood building regulations that oblige a great deal of time and expense to make administrative financial condition Contractors are enthusiastic about customary strategy in light of the fact that they are acquainted with the system. Changing strategy or exchange will require more venture to prepare the labourers, minimum or purchase hardware. Thus little builders are not intrigued by IBS.

Understanding the execution of IBS is still to make progress, CIDB through its examination arm, Construction Research Institute of Malaysia (CREAM) has taken the activity from the issue distinguished prior and kept on directing three arrangement of IBS workshops session with the business somewhere around 2006 and 2007. After an extensive pondering with the stakeholders, it was reasoned that the variables helping the postponements of IBS execution and different issues identified with IBS are absence of push component for powers and dependable government bodies by laws and regulations. The experts in Malaysia are absence of specialized learning about IBS parts

.

IBS oblige on location particular abilities for gathering and erection of parts, where there are absence of these steady experts. There is likewise absence of unique gear's and apparatus which hampered work. The confound between preparation of commercial ventures with IBS focuses by the legislature inclined to be vital. Interest from Bumiputera foremen as an erectors or produces was likewise inadequate. There is absence of building undertakings for foremen to secure extend in development.

The fundamental explanations behind the low reception of IBS in Malaysia as expressed in Construction Industry Master Plan (CIMP 2006-2015) are absence of joining in outline stage and poor information. IBS producers are at present included just after configuration stage. This absence of reconciliation among applicable players in configuration stage has resultant in requirement for arrangement upgrade and extra cost to be caused if IBS is received. Customer and sanctioning powers have poor information of IBS contrasted with engineers and architects. Nature with IBS idea and its advantages is fundamental to its prosperity in light of the fact that IBS obliges distinctive approach in development.

The hindrances of IBS usage in Malaysia can be abridged and classified in a few subjects, which are institutionalization and quality issues, issues in purchaser recognition, issues in expert observation, process and inventory network, innovation, preparing and instruction,

50

back and costing, motivator and correspondence issues.

2.12   Construction Industry Master Plan (CIMP) 2006-2015

CIDB together with the commanders of the development business have drafted.

Development Industry Master Plan (CIMP) 2006-2015. The criticalness of examination as stipulated in the Cimp's fifth Strategic Thrust is reflected in the way that it is the characterizing device to produce creativity that enhance the quality, execution and standard of the development business through R&D. The criticalness of ICT for development is clarified in Strategic Thrust 6. This push assumes huge parts in changing outline and building process in IBS from virtual to reality. The normal focus in year 2015 for Strategic Thrust 5 which gives accentuation on IBS and Strategic Thrust 6 is highlighted in Table 2.

Table 2. 5 Expected Target of CIMP Strategic Thrust 5 and Strategic Thrust 6 by year 2015

2.13   Summary

In this way, if saw decidedly, there is an incredible potential for IBS to become in the nation. By and by, the dedication and collaboration between the general population and private divisions is foremost in guaranteeing the fruitful usage of building industrialization.

Likewise, the Malaysia's development workforce is maturing and contracting as dynamically less adolescent enter the business. This sensation prompts the business to depend intensely on remote specialists. In the event that, the interest for work continues as before and the supply diminish, development expense will increment and in the end pass on this expense to the home purchasers. Thus, the industrialization of building development technique and the advancement of development innovation are inescapable and conceivable.

This segment has concentrated on some more extensive issue that could influence the take-up of industrialized building framework (IBS) in Malaysia. Notwithstanding different monetary and noneconomic profits of IBS, its usage is not generally acknowledged by the development players. Subsequently, different useful projects, for example, workshop, colloquiums, and, meetings or maybe the joint effort with the state funded colleges ought to be concocted to illuminate the private segment and additionally general society part.

There are numerous sorts of IBS existing in Malaysia: formwork precast loadbearing divider board, precast casing, precast floor and empty centre chunk, sandwich board, piece board, and steel outline. These IBS speak to a large portion of the IBS that exist around the world. Quality, rate of development, and expense reserve funds are the principle points of interest of these frameworks. These variables are vital in actualizing the Ninth Malaysia Plan. The principle weaknesses of the IBS in Malaysia are that they are exceedingly capital concentrated and there is a requirement for specialists at the development site for some of them. The primary motivation to suggest the utilization of IBS in Malaysia is that the crude materials utilized as a part of the IBS must be delivered generally keeping in mind the end goal to defeat the deficiencies that are constantly confronted by the IBS development.

RESEARCH METHODOLOGY

3.1   Introduction

Research philosophy is the technique that used to discover, gather, examinations information and along these lines giving result focused around perception. The correct arranging and point of interest study to the stream of the exploration technique is pivotal in place serves as an aide to attain the destinations and extents of the study. This section might further talk about in detail the examination techniques, from how the information is gathered till how it is prepared and broke down to accomplish the goals and extents of the study.

This part goes for explaining the methodological process that used to complete the exploration focused around the destinations of the study. This is including the writing audit furthermore the arrangement of poll keeping in mind the end goal to acquire enter that are needed.

3.2   Research Methodology

This segment of study would concentrate on the strategy for study to be done to attain the goal of this report. Hence, every measure taken must be proper and significant to the related theme of study. Three methodologies have been all through this study to assemble solid and important information. The methodologies are:

a.   Literature audit

b.   Handing out of poll

c.   Reviewing the powerful vital plan system

Figure 3. 1 Research flow chart

53

3.3   Literature Review

Writing audit is a paramount part in the study as far as social event auxiliary information. The past investigates that were carried out give critical data furthermore served as a rule so as to help better understanding of the study. Writing audit help degree down the inquires about by disposing of a ton of work that were past done by different specialists, it give as a decent rule to brought up what range required to be concentrated in this examination.

3.4   Survey

Survey is a situated of pre-formulated and composed inquiries that the scientists might want to ask to respondents and record their answers. Poll can be an effective information gathering apparatus when the scientist knows precisely on the data that is required and how to measure the variables of investment. Subsequently, all inquiries ought to be clear, justifiable and get no vagueness. Information acceptance was directed after the surveys had been gathered. At present information approval, the answers got from the surveys will be checked for exactness and suitability for this exploration reason.

3.4.1 Sampling of Data

There were around 100 duplicates of surveys conveyed to the focused on respondents. Respondents for the poll in this exploration are comprised of foremen, experts, engineers, modellers and amount surveyors in Malaysia.

Giving out poll is a methodology to focus the current boundaries of the execution of IBS that have been drilled among the development players in Malaysia. It was intended to assemble and check the data from writing audit. The technique for conveyance and gathering of the poll overview envelop the accompanying:

- ☐   Via mail and returned through mail through stamped self-tended to envelope
- ☐   By adjusting through phone calls and dispatching the survey
- ☐   By hand dispersions for chose respondents
- ☐   By email poll strategy

3.4.2 The Design of Questionnaire

Survey is a viable route intended to assemble and confirm the data which from writing studies. Notwithstanding, the limit of poll is that it is subjected to the ability and participation of the respondent in finishing the survey. Accordingly, it is important to outline the poll as direct as could be allowed to get data identified with the goals of the study. An alternate imperative measure when outlining the poll is the time to finish it. It ought to be intended to be finished in the most limited time feasible for the accommodation of the respondent as the workload of the respondents is normally substantial.

The survey comprised of five sections, general data of respondent, and a study on their experience along with preparation adjusting IBS in development undertakings, figure that influencing improvement of IBS, obstructions of adjusting IBS in development industry and in conclusion approaches to upgrade execution of IBS. Respondents were recommended to join their business cards or organization stamp to the poll structures. The data accumulated was as per the following:

Section A: General information of the respondent
- • Name of participant
- • Occupation
- • Designation
- • Job experience

Section B: Familiarity along with readiness adapting Industrialized Building System or IBS in construction developments
- • Familiarity with IBS
- • Familiarity with a mixture types of IBS
- • Readiness by means of IBS in building developments

Section C: Factor that affecting development of IBS

- • Guidelines along with Incentive

- • Excellence expectation

- • Productivity

- • Technical

- • Financial

- • Management

Section D: Barriers of adapting IBS in construction industry

- • Product support

- • Marketing

- • Funding

- • Certification

- • Sharing the Best Practices

Section E: Ways to enhance implementation of IBS

- • Incentives from government

- • Education, training and awareness

- • Standardization

- • Promotion

- • Enforcement

- • More research and development

3.5   Methods of Analysis

The data and information assembled through survey were incorporated and transformed utilizing normal list technique as a part of connection to the goals and extent of study. Two factual strategies were connected, in particular spellbinding fact and inferential facts. Result from the discoveries will be exhibited as charts, histogram and pie graph for simpler understanding.

3.5.1 Average Index

Regular index is being deliberate based on the method of:

Where, a = constant, weighing factor for i, x =
        frequency of respondent i = 1, 2, 3... n

A scale of 5 classes has been utilized for the normal list technique so as to show need. The scales of 5 classifications are:

Table 3. 1 Grad of the answers

1	Least agreed	1.00-1.50
2	Moderate	1.50-2.50
3		2.50-3.50
4	Mostly agreed	2.5-4.5
5		4.5-5.00

3.5.2 Frequency Analysis

The gathered crude information is obliged to be differentiated in a table of recurrence to demonstrate the dissemination of every information gathered.

3.5.3 Rank

Rank shows relative position or requesting when looking at the issues in the same class. Rank is focused around the normal list. Higher rank with low rank numbers unless specified generally will be for the most part have more criticalness or impacts in wording when come to examination and the other way around. It is extremely helpful with a specific end goal to highlighted and rundown out of its imperativeness.

3.5.4 Standard Deviation

In this examination, standard deviation is utilized as a measure of the variability or scattering the information set from recurrence investigation. A low standard deviation demonstrates that the information indicates tend be near the same quality (the mean), while elevated expectation deviation shows that the information are spread out over a substantial scope of qualities. It is utilized to confirm the example and dissemination of the gathered information that aid in while doing examinations in regarded class.

3.5.5 Comments

Remarks come in situational which are order of the broke down information that focused around the normal lists, positions, and standard deviations of the information. It turns the numbers in the examinations to more compelling expressions that could be translated less demanding by others.

3.6 Summary of Chapter

This chapter describes in detail the flow of the study from the initial stage to the end in achieving the objectives. The choices of the methods used is highly depends on the study. For this study, questionnaire survey is used to gather the data of the study and percentage analysis are used to analyse the data collected. In other hand we can said this can be most important part of project and also so useful for other parts of the structure.

ANALYSIS AND DISCUSSION

4.1   Introduction

This section concentrates on breaking down the results assembled from the respondents through meeting and survey. Since time distributed for the dissemination and gathering of the survey is exceptionally restricted, the circulation of poll is constrained to the respondents inside the scope of the scientist just.

The information gathered were changed over into more genuine, helpful and enlightening arrangements that are as tables and figures. The information likewise were communicated as indicated by the suitability of the investigation itself. The polls were circulated into diverse parts empowers the investigation be carried out deliberately and reflects an intelligent result.

4.2 Distributions and Return of the Questionnaire

There were around 100 duplicates of surveys were appropriated to the focused on respondents comprised of engineers, foremen, designers, advisors and amount surveyors. By the cut-off date, the analyst figured out how to gather back 30 useable polls from the respondents. This constitute of a whole of 30 percent reaction rate. As per Fellows et al (1997), the ordinary expected useable reaction rate is going from 25 percent to 35 percent. Subsequently, the aggregate reaction got is viewed as sufficient with the end goal of this exploration.

The return rate of the conveyed survey is as demonstrated in Figure 4.1. From Figure 4.1, it is demonstrated the return rates of the surveys were run from 25 percent to 40 percent. In this exploration, the information gathered by utilizing email and self-gather system secure a higher return rate than other dispersion strategy. Surveys were sent via email to respondents who worked in the development business. Other than that, the specialist additionally makes a couple of visits to development firms around the neighbourhood appropriate the survey by hand. This strategy is abate as the appropriation is restricted and the separation starting with one then onto the next spot is far. Be that as it may, appropriation of survey by postal have much lower reaction rate than the other system.

Bar Chart 4. 1 Return Percentage of Questionnaire by the Respondents

4.3 Question Structure

The example of the poll can be alluded in Appendix A. The poll is separated into five areas as depicted in Chapter 3. The examination predominantly cantered into three sections as talked about as takes after:

4.4 Respondent information
4.4.1 Respondent Distribution

Chart 4. 1 Collected returns of usable questionnaires

Figure 4.2 demonstrates the returned useable surveys of the diverse sorts of respondents in the development business. 43 percent out of 30 useable polls were from builders, which speak to the biggest gatherings of reaction in this exploration. Foremen give significant data as they are the individuals who manage the bleeding edge of the development. They are the individuals who face issues in this aggressive development industry. Accordingly, the result from these respondents would give a reasonable diagram of current level of usage of IBS in the Malaysian development industry.

4.4.2 Respondent Position

Alluding to Figure 4.3 shows diverse level of position of the respondents in the development business. A large portion of the respondent is from the specialized level who in charge of the general specialized work of the firm. The engineer/ Architect/ amount surveyor/ other specialized staff comprise of 34 percent of the aggregate respondents. This gathering of respondents is the bleeding edge of the individuals who in contact with the outline phase of the development ventures. Their notions are extremely helpful and give genuine experiences to this examination. Other than that the other top related managerial work force and administration level faculty additionally can give profitable data to the examination.

Chart 4. 2 Current Position of Respondents in Construction Industry

4.4.3 Respondent Experience in Construction Industry

Figure 4.4 and Figure 4.5 represents knowledge of the development business and knowledge of the development business separately. In Figure 4.4, the respondents chiefly have more than ten years of involvement in development industry (47 percent). Indistinguishably, Figure 4.5 shows a large portion of their development firms (60 percent) likewise have more than ten years of involvement in development industry.

Chart 4. 3 Respondent Experience in Construction Industry

Chart 4. 4 Construction Company Experience in Construction Industry

4.5   Readiness of adapting IBS in construction projects

4.5.1 Experience of IBS in Construction Industry

The principle stage to recognize the status of conforming IBS being developed wanders is to perceive the respondent contribution with IBS. There are four parameters to be tended to here as presented in Table 4.1.

4.5.1.1 Knowledge in IBS

The essential request is to recognize their understanding with the terms IBS previous of this investigation. At that point the second question is to assess their certified data with IBS. From the overviews diagram examination, the result exhibits that fair around 37 percent of the respondents consider IBS prior of the survey (by considering respondents that pick answer 4 and 5). There are 27 percent of the respondents having alongside zero intimation what truly does IBS suggests (respondents that pick answer 1 or 2). The examination to this 27 percent of respondents that fit in with this characterization are further analyzed to relate it with the general information of the respondent. This examination is further spoken to in Figure 4.6.

Table 4. 1 Respondent Experience with IBS

Figure 4.6 exhibit that all the C&s specialists have typical or extraordinary data in IBS. Meanwhile 38 percent of the manufacturers have little or low data in IBS, which is seen as the most essential in this examination. The "creator" get-together is not considered in this examination in light of the way that the data got from the example size is not sufficient to make legitimate examination. From this figure shows that the advancement players that included in the design process i.e. expert and specialists have higher data with IBS appeared differently in relation to the people who does excluded in arrangement process, which are the developers and originators.

Bar Chart 4. 2 Knowledge of IBS according to their profession

4.5.1.2 Experiences in IBS

The third bit of Table 4.1 is to break down the information of the respondent in using IBS as a piece of their building endeavours. Table 4.1 exhibits that larger piece of the respondents for this examination with ordinary document 2.30 has low level of learning of using IBS as a piece of advancement industry. There are only 10 percent of the respondent have incredible or amazing foundation of using IBS as a piece of the improvement business. The last part for Table 4.1 shows that in abundance of 76 percent of the respondents have experiences in less than five advancement wanders that usage IBS.

4.6   Respondent experience with types of IBS

Table 4.2 demonstrates the respondent involvement with sorts of IBS. By and large, the general involvement with each one kind of IBS is at low level with normal list range from 2.13 to 2.77. This can be delegated „poor" and „below average" as in Table 4.2.

Respondents have more encounters in piece work framework and steel outline structures and top trusses.

The most well-known sorts of IBS in the development ventures in this examination is the piece work framework which have normal file of 2.77. Such framework uses square work to wipe out the employments of segment and bar in basic single story of building for instance of open toilets and utilities.

The second most normal sort is fortified solid structures with precast solid section which has normal record 2.47. Such frameworks are otherwise called crossover framework in light of the fact that it utilizes ordinary system and precast sections. In some circumstance this system are turn out to be more convenient where the ventures does not bear to include in the volume that empowers altered sort of precast segments and pillars. The employments of precast chunks which come in standard structure component and sizes enormously decrease the time and work required to be performed in site particularly for those customer driven quick track venture like Tesco and Jusco and so on.

Table 4. 2 Respondent experience with types of IBS

Prefabricated timber framing system and steel formwork system have the lowest score which average index of 2.13. The economic factor of timber system has drawn back the usability of such system. Meanwhile the steel formwork system is yet to gain popularity in Malaysia as the timber formwork is a cheaper option and solution to most construction projects.

On the whole, the implementation of IBS in the construction projects is at poor level which being expressed in average index of less than 2.80. The confidence level for the respondents answering these questionnaires is at poor level. IBS involves high construction cost, high degree of repetition, lack of awareness and involving skilled workers to install the system itself that may require much expertise and might be expensive at the same time.

4.7   Readiness of using IBS in building projects

Table 4.3 shows the readiness of adapting IBS in building projects. The readiness of adapting IBS is considered as average as shown in Table 4.3. The respondents feel that they were most prepared in term of labour if considering of each sub section, which average index achieve 3.67. This is followed by material which has the average index of 3.60. The respondents are most prepared in these two categories.

Table 4. 3 Readiness of using IBS in building projects

Meanwhile the readiness of using IBS is in terms of technical knowledge having the lowest rank in this survey. This shows that what highlighted in Construction Industry Master Plan (CIMP 2006-2015) is true where poor technical knowledge is one of the main reasons for the low adoption of IBS in Malaysia. This lead to lack of integration caused IBS manufacturers involved only after the design stage. This lack of integration among relevant players in design stage has resultant in need for plan redesign and additional cost to be incurred if IBS is adopted. In this research also pointed out where architects tend to have lower experiences with various types of IBS than contractors and engineers.

4.8   Factors affecting the development of IBS

The factors affecting the development of IBS are as discussed in Table 4.4. There are six categories of factors as pointed out by Iwani (2008) and each of the categories has its own breakdown factors as shown in Table 4.4. The different method of approaches is used in this research compared with what that has been conducted in previous research. The most important factors affecting development of IBS is the good quality control and the speed of construction that IBS provide. Besides that, the respondent believe that certification of products, process and people is the second most important factors in implementing IBS in the construction industry. Meanwhile, attractiveness of potential margins and incentives in increase of government project using IBS is also the other important factors in implementation of IBS.

The heavily mechanised approach has displeased a substantial number of the labour force from the building construction industry. IBS is a tremendous need for expert labour at the construction site. Therefore extra costs are needed to train the semiskilled labour force for highly skilled jobs. The main reasons for delay in early completion of projects in IBS construction industry are supply delay, bad weather, and shortage of raw material. In some cases, the main reason for the delay was the lack of labour experience. This is because certain types of IBS construction are still new in Malaysia and the labour force is still not familiar with the special erection procedure required by those systems.

4.9   Barriers in the implementation of IBS in construction industry

For this research, the barriers of adapting IBS in construction industry were divided into five categories as shown in Table 4.5. In these categories, the most identifiable category is funding which have average index of 3.70. The least influential barriers is the marketing category which of 3.35.

Table 4. 5 Barriers in the implementation of IBS in construction industry

Table 4.6 drilled down the primary hindrances of embracing IBS in development industry. As indicated by the information investigation, the level of institutionalization of IBS item is the most compelling boundaries in the usage of IBS. Adjustment of institutionalization obliges an enormous training and preparing exertion.

Institutionalization of building components face safety from development industry due to the style reservation and financial reasons (Kampempool et al, 1986). Rahman et al (2006) says that the cost of IBS is not aggressive on the grounds that absence of backing from

65

government supported task, which positioned second in the hindrances of IBS usage in this examination.

Evaluate 4.8 recorded the five most compelling boundaries and five minimum powerful obstructions. From the figure, it is to demonstrate that the functional restrictions are liable to have more impacts to the boundaries of IBS usage in the development business. Then again, the backhanded constraints are likely have less impacts to the hindrances of IBS execution in the development business.

Table 4. 6 Barriers in the implementation of IBS in construction industry (in categories)

Score	Frequency Analysis					Average Index	Std Dev	Rank
	1	2	3	4	5			
Product support								
Manufacturer not keen t proceed with IBS concep	(	3	'	18	2	3.63	0.76	7
Material not fully exploited		2	1	11	3	3.43	0.90	14
Price	(	3	'	9	9	3.80	1.00	2
Requires information sharing/database on tool & machines	(	3	'	12	6	3.70	0.92	6
Level of standardization		0	:	13	8	3.90	0.92	1
Compatibility and dema	(	6	(	12	6	3.60	1.04	9
Marketing								
Product driver	(	8	1	7	3	3.17	0.95	20
Industry marketing strategies	:	3	1	6	5	3.30	1.09	18
Market Security	(	5	1	9	4	3.40	0.92	16

						Mean	SD	Rank
Educate the contractor available to apply IBS		7		9	4	3.20	1.16	19
Market Demand		4	1	7	7	3.50	1.11	12
Funding								
Obtaining finance		3		11	7	3.73	0.94	5
Initial cost and whole life		4		9	7	3.57	1.10	10
Government fund projec		3		15	6	3.80	0.89	2
Certification								
Lack of knowledge		4	1	13	3	3.50	0.86	12
Restrictive regulations		2	1	11	3	3.43	0.90	14
Technical limitation		3		11	8	3.80	0.96	2
Sharing the Best Practice								
Expertise		2	1	11	5	3.63	0.85	7
User satisfaction		6		12	3	3.40	0.93	16
Skill shortage		2	1	15	2	3.57	0.73	10

Bar Chart 4. 3 Barriers in the implementation of IBS in construction industry

4.10 Ways to enhance implementation of IBS

Table 4.7 demonstrates a percentage of the conceivable approaches to improve usage of IBS. The respondent concurred that delicate courses, for example, more impetuses, evidence cost and time reserve funds and backings from the legislatures are much superior to hard routes, for example, uphold IBS with law, strict regulations and bar shoddy work.

Hussein (2007) highlighted the expenses of utilizing IBS surpass the customary strategy for development due to shoddy settler work. IBS outline idea not being looked into in development venture. Fashioners did not outline utilizing parts as they not find the segments in the business sector, whilst makers won't deliver parts as they don't see configuration utilizing parts. *Table 4. 7 Ways to enhance implementation of IBS*

Customer desire on the quality and configuration has stood out to hunt down more cost effective, amazing and quicker conveyance frameworks. The current observation is that customarily manufactured development compares to building life span. The legislature needs to go about as the key driver to encourage future improvement. One of the key advantages of IBS is the capacity to make separation in configuration requiring little to no effort. The framework ought to be effectively adaptable to empower be talked outline, promptly versatile to suit singular necessities.

4.11 Discussion

There are numerous difficulties in the actualizing of IBS in the current condition of the development businesses in light of the fact that it includes numerous gatherings, for example, material suppliers, work, sub foremen and others will be influenced. In spite of the fact that IBS has been presented for more than twenty years, however the development still applies the customary which has been demonstrated filthy, unsafe and inefficient. Accordingly there must be a system detailed to empower the application of IBS in the nearby development industry. Followings are some discourse raised focused around the investigation of the study.

4.11.1 Reliance on manpower

Labour is a standout amongst the most pressing difficulties confronting the Malaysian development industry as the "wet exchange" development approach at present depends vigorously on the accessibility of countless specialists. The "wet exchange" development approach implied is the customary cast in situ strategy. Obviously, the development business in Malaysia is exceptionally relies on upon the labour particularly outside works. This is on account of the business is additionally ready to utilize incompetent remote works with less expensive rates.

4.11.2 Avoid mismatch between the roadmap and readiness among contractors and designers

This exploration called attention to that development players are arranged regarding materials and work to adjust IBS, yet absence of specialized learning and configuration norms are the disadvantages. Absence of past involvement in IBS and their expert is absence of specialized information in IBS has for the most part disheartened IBS to take up (Hamid et al., 2008). Instead of to say they are unwilling to transform, they are not able to change. Regardless of that different government plans, guides, endeavours, for example, IBS Roadmap 2003-2010, CIMP 2006-2015 and so forth to help on usage of IBS, it is likewise vital to guarantee that such deliberations does not makes a difference with the uncalled for routes among the builders and designers.

4.11.3 Barriers of implementing IBS to various parties in construction

The exploration additionally brought up the fundamental hindrances in receiving IBS are essentially in view of level of institutionalization is inadequate, value, absence of backing from government financed ventures and specialized limits.

To customers and builders, unless there was important quick track activities, for example, Tesco, Jusco venture, IBS is regularly confused as high hazard and extravagant arrangement (Kamarul, 2009). To planners which are the designers and specialists, absence of learning among the IBS originators helps postpones in configuration stage, for instance architects require additional time to create subtle elements attracting to cook the utilization of IBS segments in their outline.

An alternate boundary is in managing made engineers. There are the hardest to persuade to utilize IBS contrasted with more modest and less settled modellers. For them, work must take after structure. However in IBS, it is the other route around (IBS Modular Sdn. Bhd, 2009).

4.11.4 The Ways of Implementing IBS

In this exploration, the results could be divided into soft ways and hard ways to actualize IBS in Malaysian development industry. Soft ways, for example, more impetuses, confirmation cost and time investment funds and backings from the legislatures has a tendency to get more consideration from the respondents. Then again, the hard ways, for example, uphold IBS with law, strict regulations and bar shabby work can be viewed as less proficient and may bring antagonistic impact to the construction Industry.

CONCLUSIONS AND RECOMMENDATIONS

5.1 Conclusions

This point of the examination is to inspect and study the boundaries in present advancement of IBS in Malaysian development industry. The reason for this part is to finish up all the discoveries got from the study. All the three targets set for the examination have been effectively attained and the discoveries are condensed focused around the goals of the exploration as takes after:

5.1.1 Objective

1: To identify readiness of contractors and designers to adapt IBS in their construction projects.

2: To determine barriers in the implementation of IBS in Malaysian construction industry.

3: To identify ways to enhance the implementation of IBS in the construction industry.

This goal is to distinguish the availability of the development players to adjust IBS in their development venture. From the discoveries, the level of general status of the development players is at normal level just. The status regarding work and material to receive IBS is higher than others figure. Then again the preparation regarding specialized information is low. All the elements above are singularly focused around the respondents" encounters since they are included in the application of IBS in the lodging advancement ventures. There are numerous different elements that can be considered as more variables help the more refined brings about the examinations.

The obstructions of receiving IBS in Malaysian development industry is principally because of absence of institutionalization of IBS segment, high cost of IBS item, specialized impediment, absence of backing from government subsidized tasks to private part. The minimum most compelling hindrances are showcasing methodologies and item driver.

The strategic management process does not end when the strategy has been decided to pursue and therefore there must be a translation the strategy into action. There must be a commitment and the strategy implementation effort by all the parties involved. The success of the strategy formulation does not contribute to the successful implementation of the strategy. Implementing strategies require such action such as altering the laws, acts and legislations, training workers and others.

Soft ways such as more incentives, proof cost and time savings and supports from the governments are some of the good way to further enhance the usage of IBS in construction industry. However the hard ways such as enforce IBS with law, strict regulations and bar cheap labour is considered least favourable by the respondents, therefore is not efficient and could bring adverse effect to the industry.

5.2   Recommendations

This finding of the study gives a viable methodology to actualize IBS in the current condition of the development business. In any case, there are still a few ranges in the IBS administration that can be research to lead an examination which can be investigate for further studies and further change can be made. The accompanying suggestion can be considered and utilized as reference for future study purposes.

1.   Implementation arrangement of IBS by presenting approach and rules for compelling execution

2.   Investigation on configuration coordination issues in IBS and traditional venture

3.   Continuous change that on the part of enhancing the methodology of actualizing IBS

4.   Financial viewpoint as in the credit and the payback framework to support IBS interests in keeping money framework

5.   CSF or Critical Success Factors in the usage of IBS in broad daylight and private

71

ventures in Malaysia

There are truly a quantities of study related on IBS has been directed all through Malaysia since 1996. The reason for these overviews is to accumulate data on execution and application of IBS structures Malaysia. IBS characteristics potential development framework for the future with accentuation on quality, higher benefit and less work escalated. Other than the point of progressively diminishing the reliance on outside work and sparing the country's misfortune in remote trade, IBS gives the chance to the players in the development business to extend another picture of the business to be at standard with other assembling based industry, for example, the auto and electronic commercial ventures. The reception of IBS guarantees to lift each level of the development business to new statures and picture of professionalism. IBS ought to be seen as the advanced techniques for development where cutting edge and methodical strategies for outline, generation arranging and automated routines for assembling and erection are connect.

REFERENCES

Badir, Kadi,Ali , YF, MRA,AAA, 1998. *Building system classification. Bulletin of Institute of Engineer*. 1st ed. Malaysia: A.A.A.

Bing, L., Kwong, Hao, L, YW, KJ, 2001. *Seismic behaviour of connection between precast concrete beams*. 1st ed. Bulletin: CSE Research.

Buddhi, ss, 2004. *Civil Computing Computer Applications in Civil Engineering*. 2nd ed. Thailand: Academic Press.

Abbas Karami, A.M, 2005. *Implementaion of IBS in all over the world*. 1st ed. USA: Abaddon Books.

CIDB, A.M, 2003. *Industrialised Building Systems*. 1st ed. Malaysia: CIDB.

Hamid, Kamar, Ghani, Z, K.A.M, A.H.A, 2008. *Industrialized Building System (IBS) in Malaysia*. 1st ed. Malaysia: the current state and R&D initiatives.

, 2004. *Globalization: Culture and Education in the New Millennium*. 0 Edition. University of California Press.

Thomas Lockwood, 2008. *Building Design Strategy: Using Design to Achieve Key Business Objectives*. 1 Edition. Allworth Press.

Design Museum, 2010. *How To Design a House (Design Museum How to)*. 1St Edition Edition. Conran.

JÃ1/4rgen Adam, 2004. *Industrial Buildings (Design Manuals)*. 1 Edition. Birkhäuser Architecture.

Roy Chudley, 2014. *Building Construction Handbook*. 10 Edition. Routledge.

Carles Broto, 2015. *Apartment Building: Design and Innovation*. Edition. Links International,Ceg.

Dietz, A.G.H .S .CIDB , 2003. Industrialized Building System. 1st ed. Malaysia: Academic Press.

Din Esa, H, 1984. Industrialized building and its application. 1st ed. Malaysia: amazon.

APPENDIX

Questionnaire on Barriers of IBS in Malaysia

The objectives of this questionnaire are:

-To identify readiness of contractors and designers to adapt IBS in their construction projects.

-To determine barriers in implementation of IBS in Malaysian construction.

-To identify ways to enhance the implementation of IBS in construction industry.

All data will be kept confidential and used anonymously for research purpose only.

Researcher:

SAEED KAMANKESH

Linton University College

Email: saeed_kamankesh@yahoo.com

Questionnaire

Section A: General information of the respondent

- Name of participant
- Occupation
- Designation
- Job experience

Section B: Familiarity along with readiness adapting Industrialized Building System or IBS in construction developments

- Familiarity with IBS
- Familiarity with a mixture types of IBS
- Readiness by means of IBS in building developments

Section C: Factor that affecting development of IBS

- Guidelines along with Incentive
- Excellence expectation
- Productivity
- Technical
- Financial
- Management

Section D: Barriers of adapting IBS in construction industry

- Product support
- Marketing

- ➢ Funding
- ➢ Certification
- ➢ Sharing the Best Practices

Section E: Ways to enhance implementation of IBS

- ➢ Incentives from government
- ➢ Education, training and awareness
- ➢ Standardization
- ➢ Promotion
- ➢ Enforcement
- ➢ More research and development

www.ingramcontent.com/pod-product-compliance
Lightning Source LLC
Chambersburg PA
CBHW051229200326
41519CB00025B/7305